CAROLYN COKER ROSS, MD, MPH

Healing Body, Mind and Spirit

An Integrative Medicine Approach
to the Treatment of Eating Disorders

Outskirts Press, Inc.
Denver, Colorado

Outskirts Press
http://www.outskirtspress.com

ISBN-10: 1-4327-0191-6
ISBN-13: 978-1-4327-0191-8

"Dr. Carolyn Ross writes with the wisdom and expertise of a clinician who has worked extensively in the areas of mental health, eating disorders and weight management, seamlessly weaving the best of conventional and complementary medicine."

Tieraona Low Dog, MD
Director of Education
Program in Integrative Medicine
University of Arizona Health Sciences Department

"Dr. Ross's Integrative Approach to eating disorder treatment is clearly and observably effective. I have never met anyone who exceeded her commitment to her patients both while they are under her care and well into their aftercare experience. Her patients frequently express their first sense of hopefulness at the awakening of mind, body and spirit that is addressed in Dr. Ross's method."

Dr. Barbara Cole
Author: *The Eating Disorder Solution*
Clinical Director, Victorian House

"Dr. Carolyn Ross is a highly skilled physician, but better yet, she is a humane, compassionate human being who possesses a healing influence tied to her wisdom, intuition and authenticity as a woman. Her integrative approach to the treatment of eating disorders is innovative and effective and truly offers the possibility of healing of body, mind and spirit."

Wendy Oliver-Pyatt, MD
Director, Center for Hope of the Sierras
Asst. Professor of Psychiatry, University of Nevada Medical School

ACKNOWLEDGEMENTS

My life has been blessed by many mentors who have helped me grow both professionally and personally. I am very grateful to Andrew Weil, M.D., Victoria Maizes, M.D., Randy Horowitz, M.D., Tieraona Lowdog, M.D. and the other members of the faculty at the Program in Integrative Medicine at the University of Arizona, where I first began to see the broader applicability of Integrative Medicine.

I cannot express my gratitude enough to the members of the Eating Disorders program team that I have the pleasure to work with and to my medical director, Dr. Michael Scott. Without this supportive structure, I would never have been able to express my creativity and implement the integrative medicine approach spoken of in this book. Particular thanks go to lead therapist Jeannette Rojas, family therapist Barbara Sullivan and dietician Lee Roach who have kept me going and encouraged me with their support.

I must also acknowledge my three sons, Dutch and Noah Ross and Sammy Legge. Sammy has borne the brunt of my long hours at work and more long hours at home writing and editing. Dutch has encouraged me and supported me through some dark nights of the soul. Noah's spirit is what prompted my entry into the field of mental illness. As I watched his long battle with depression and subsequent death, I made a sacred vow to find options for other mother's children with mental illness in the hopes that a few may live longer and more productive lives. The cover photo taken by Noah speaks to his talent and the tragedy of a life cut short.

TABLE OF CONTENTS

INTRODUCTION

"I eat and eat and I know that I should stop, but I can't. I've eaten so much that I throw up, my stomach hurts, and I have to lie down. Sometimes, I feel like if I don't eat everything I can get my hands on, I will explode." *Binge Eater*

"There was so much blood when I went to the bathroom that I thought I was on my period. Later I found out I was bleeding from my rectum because of all the laxatives I'd used. I had to stop the laxatives because I was dizzy and light-headed. So I just stopped eating. I would allow myself to drink one diet soda per day. I didn't eat any solid foods. I didn't deserve anything else. I hate my body. I feel disgusted by it. I just want to disappear, to be invisible." *Anorexic*

"When purging stopped working and I felt so fat, I increased my use of cocaine. When I used coke, I felt the same power I used to feel when I first started bingeing and purging. I could go for days without eating. I could work out for three hours at a time. I lost weight. When I couldn't get coke, I would purge as many as ten times a day. I had to get everything out. After purging, I felt high, on top of the world, and then I would crash again into the shame and guilt of having done something so disgusting." *Bulimic*

These stories illustrate some of the behaviors and thinking patterns across the spectrum of eating disorders. While there are many differences in the superficial behaviors of these patients, there are also some **commonalities:**

- the driving compulsion to be thin at all costs;
- the fixation on external appearance to the exclusion of all else;
- the emotional vicious circle ending in shame, guilt, and self-loathing;
- attempts to control these uncontrollable urges; and, most importantly,
- *the unhealthy relationship with food and attempts to deal with emotional distress through abstaining from food or overeating.*

Conventional approaches to the treatment of eating disorders focus on the management of medical consequences and the use of psychopharmacology. Cognitive behavioral therapies target eating disorder symptoms such as purging, bingeing, restricting, etc. With this approach, about one-half of patients will get well, one-fourth will have a remitting and relapsing course, and the remainder will get worse or die. What does a whole-person or integrative medicine approach add? Why should one even consider this approach?

There is sparse data on the use of complementary and alternative medicine (CAM) therapies in eating disorder patients. However, there are studies that show CAM use by patients with psychiatric diagnoses in general is high. There is also information specific to the use of CAM therapies for diagnoses such as depression and anxiety that are comorbid with eating disorders. Use of any CAM therapy is greater among persons who are diagnosed with psychiatric disorders than the general population. These same patients also use conventional therapies. Patients diagnosed with severe depression or anxiety use CAM therapies most often.[1] One survey of patients seen at a psychiatric clinic found that 54 percent used some type of CAM therapy for psychiatric and/or physical symptoms. Herbal remedies were the most common. Eighty-nine percent reported some improvement in their psychiatric symptoms.[2] Relaxation techniques and spiritual healing are the most commonly used CAM therapies for those diagnosed with depression and anxiety specifically. Data from a nationally representative sample of patients with anxiety and/or depression in the United States showed that 56.7 percent of those with anxiety attacks and 53.6 percent of those with severe depression used complementary and alternative therapies to treat their depression or anxiety.[3]

Conventional treatments for eating disorders and for conditions comorbid with eating disorders such as depression have limited efficacy. At least 30 percent of patients diagnosed with depression and treated with conventional therapies do not respond, and increasing dosages of medication often cause more side effects. This is one of the reasons why CAM therapies have been increasing in popularity with consumers and with physicians. Reported use of CAM increased 25 percent between 1990 and 1997, mostly due to increases in the number of patients seeking CAM therapies, not more visits per patient[4] (Eisenberg, 1999). Many physicians state that they believe that CAM therapies are valid (acupuncture 51 percent, chiropractic 53 percent, massage 48 percent, homeopathy 26 percent, and herbal medicine 13 percent). Forty-three percent of conventionally trained physicians refer patients to acupuncture, 40 percent refer to chiropractors, and 21 percent refer to massage therapists.

The integrative medicine approach to healing body, mind, and spirit is showing promise in an inpatient program that treats the full spectrum of eating disorders. What is this approach? Why might it be successful when other types of treatment are not?

Integrative medicine is defined as healing-oriented medicine that takes into account the whole person: body, mind, and spirit, including all aspects of lifestyle. It emphasizes the therapeutic relationship and makes use of both conventional and alternative therapies. Healing of body, mind, and spirit requires not only the use of alternative therapies, but also a shift in the philosophical underpinnings of the treatment of eating disorders. Rather than focusing on the symptoms of the eating disorder and treating patients for depression, anxiety, obsessive-compulsive disorder, or concomitant drug and alcohol abuse, it is important to treat the underlying root causes and origins of the behaviors. These root causes usually began in childhood when a child's needs were not met in some way or the child was neglected or not nurtured. The child must develop some way of coping with his or her situation in life. Coping behaviors such as isolating, hiding, or walling oneself off from frightening emotions such as fear, anger, shame, or guilt make perfect sense to the child. These strategies become counterproductive in later life. The coping mechanisms that once helped the child to survive now squelch self-expression and require constant "control" maneuvers. For example, a boy who is eight when his father dies is not mature enough to deal with the enormity of his sadness and grief. He may withdraw and build up a wall that holds his overwhelming emotions at bay. Other experiences and their attendant emotions will most likely also be walled up. At some point, the strategy of walling up his feelings is not enough and he again begins to feel some of these pent-up emotions. He may choose other unhealthy coping strategies such as overeating or drinking alcohol to keep this pain at bay. All of these unhealthy coping methods have their own consequences: weight gain, depression induced by alcohol use, and others. So, what kept the little boy from feeling overwhelming pain in the moment of his father's death in later life requires a great deal of effort to suppress, also suppressing expression of his authentic or true self.

Beneath these behaviors and the emotions and physical sensations from which they "protect" the person lie core beliefs that are formed in an instant as a result of trauma, abuse, or neglect. These beliefs solidify in the psyche and, like water to fish, are no longer known or acknowledged consciously. All of these survival constructs are coping mechanisms to gain control or fill the void, establishing a pattern that stays intact until overcome by the powerful deeper urges of the soul. The soul seeks primarily one thing: self-expression, the very thing that threatens the survival of the embattled child. The boy whose father died may have been given support for his feelings of sadness and loss initially, but perhaps because of other stressors in the family, he is at some point expected to "be strong." He may form the core belief that showing emotions means you're weak. The core beliefs formed in such circumstances often promote the disease behaviors (eating disorders, drug addiction, etc.). Because they are not conscious, they can become a significant barrier that continues to "pop up" unconsciously and keep people from achieving their goal of sobriety from drugs or alcohol or abstinence from their eating disorder. The very thing that is the hardest thing for a person to do (because of an unconscious core belief) is the thing he or she must do to get well. For example, learning healthy emotional expression is essential to a strong recovery program, and this can be blocked by the core belief that to express one's emotions is a sign of weakness.

CHAPTER 1
WHY EATING DISORDERS AREN'T ENTIRELY ABOUT FOOD

"If you want a quick way to see how people relate to God, watch the way they eat." Brother Allan, O.H.C.

"To eat is human, to digest, divine." Charles T. Copeland[5]

This chapter provides a deeper understanding of the "building blocks" of eating disorders: the superficial diagnosis, the emotional soup, the sensate layer of expression, the core beliefs, and the deeper urges of the soul. These layers of personal expression contribute to and drive the engine of eating disorders.

E*mma* * *was like a deer caught in the headlights of a semi bearing down on a dark stretch of barren highway. Her hand movements when she talked were rapid and disordered, as was her speech. Her body had an athletic build and appeared tense, taut, as if she wanted to spring up from the chair in my office and run away from whatever demons haunted her. Her story was full of contradictions. She was a*

---

* Cases cited in this book have been modified: names have been changed and cases may be composites of histories from more than one patient to protect patient privacy.

heavy drinker, drinking ten or more beers every night and more on the weekends. She used over a gram of cocaine daily and thrown into that mix was abuse of amphetamines several times a week. She described her bulimia as being out of control, with episodes of bingeing and self-induced vomiting up to five times per day. She was taking several prescription medications to control her anxiety and depression. She told me: "I can't go on like this anymore." Given all of this and what I was to learn later in my work with her, I couldn't figure out how she'd held it together for as long as she had. She was a student in a high-powered graduate program on the East Coast working on her master's in social work. I wasn't as surprised at her choice of profession as much as I was that she was able to maintain a 4.0 GPA given her drug use and bulimia.

Emma's recent breakup with her boyfriend of two years triggered her admission to our inpatient eating disorder program. She cried as she told me how her drug addiction and eating disorder had caused the breakup. "I thought I had it under control. But Mark found out I was using again and he couldn't take it anymore."

Emma's mother was an alcoholic who drank heavily throughout all of Emma's childhood and was drinking still. Her parents had divorced when she was eight years old, and this was a pivotal time in her life. After the divorce, Emma was left to take care of herself and deal with her mother and a stepfather who sexually abused her between the ages of nine and thirteen. In high school, she was date raped. Unless Emma could heal the trauma and rape and neglect, it would be difficult if not impossible for her to stop pushing down her emotions with bingeing or purging when they overwhelmed her.

Emma had survived the neglect of an alcoholic mother, the abuse of her stepfather, and a date rape without telling anyone. Many patients with eating disorders have hidden trauma or neglect somewhere in their past and are in need of healing for their body, mind, and spirit. Without dealing with deep wounds such as those that Emma suffered, without identifying the root cause of the behaviors that are so obviously self-destructive, true healing of body, mind, and spirit cannot occur. Emma's depression and anxiety had been treated with medications. She had been in outpatient therapy for several years. Yet she continued to experience and to suffocate emotions of rage, shame, guilt, and fear associated with the trauma and neglect she suffered as a young child. What had changed in her? How had she coped? Why was she not able to "cope" any longer? The delicate balance in Emma's life was upset by the breakup with her boyfriend, which then unleashed many of the emotions she had been numbing herself from with drugs and her eating disorder. This event led to her being admitted for treatment and began her personal journey toward healing body, mind and spirit.

Healing body, mind, and spirit in this integrative medicine approach to treating eating disorders requires not only the use of different therapies. A philosophical shift is the underpinning of this approach and starts with an understanding of how to help those with eating disorders get to the root causes and to heal at this level first.

Diagram: Process of Recovery

1st SUPERFICIAL LEVEL OF BEHAVIORS: Eating Disorders, Substance Use, Depression, Anxiety, Sexual Compulsivity, others.

↓

2nd EMOTIONAL SOUP: Shame, Fear, Anger, Joy, Guilt – emotions in control of the person. Emotions are the fuel for behaviors.

↓

3rd SENSATE LEVEL: The body sensations associated with emotions.

$\downarrow$

4th CORE BELIEFS: Beliefs formed in the midst of intense emotion; they are often forgotten, but unconsciously these beliefs continue to shape and drive behaviors.

$\downarrow$

5th DEEPER URGES OF THE SOUL: The authentic or true self camouflaged by all of the above; Passion or Bliss. Your soul's desires.

Healing body, mind, and spirit in eating disorders requires understanding the layers of dis-ease: the superficial level of behaviors that patients are running from but are stuck in; the sensate level or bodily sensations from which patients are completely cut off; the core beliefs formed in moments of great emotion and now forgotten; and the deeper urges of the soul, struggling for expression.

Healing body, mind, and spirit in eating disorders requires understanding the layers of dis-ease: the superficial level of behaviors that patients are running from but are stuck in; the sensate level or bodily sensations from which patients are completely cut off; the core beliefs formed in moments of great emotion and now forgotten; and the deeper urges of the soul, struggling for expression.

Superficial Level of Behaviors

What we see when patients present for treatment are the superficial behaviors that have become severe enough to catch their attention or the attention of their family and friends. They may be starving themselves and / or binge eating with or without compensatory self-induced vomiting. They leave the dinner table early or make excuses to take a separate car so they can purge whatever they have eaten. They run up credit cards with the exorbitant amount of binge foods they consume. Or they become rail thin, their faces the skeletal death mask of anorexia. They may use drugs or drink to excess. Sometimes the drugs are in the service of their drive to be thinner and thinner. Or, drinking and drugging serve to make them numb and keep the feelings at bay. They may exercise three hours a day, sometimes going to the gym or running at 3 am to avoid scrutiny. Often they are so weak that they may have to reduce their exercise because of shortness of breath and fatigue. Every day, their minds are preoccupied with thoughts of how they look, how much or how little they should eat, fear of getting fat, and thoughts of self-hatred and disgust about their appearance. Often these thoughts occupy 100 percent of their daily lives, crowding out all thoughts that are not in the service of the eating disorder. As these behaviors progress, they become more isolated, losing friends and relationships as these take a backseat to their preoccupation with the eating disorder. These behaviors are what bring someone suffering from an eating disorder to treatment, but they are only the beginning of understanding the deeper root causes.

Emotional Soup

Beneath the superficial layer of behaviors is a boiling cauldron of unexposed and suppressed emotions. It is important to focus on getting to the root causes of the "disease" of which the eating disorder is a symptom. Underlying the behaviors of eating disorders and their associated comorbid diagnoses such as substance use disorder or depression or anxiety is the emotional landscape that patients are trying so desperately to avoid, escape, or suppress. This emotional layer is often confusing for patients to sort through as was the case with Bethany:

Bethany was admitted for treatment of bulimia nervosa that had come to light during a three-month hospitalization at a well-known medical hospital for treatment of severe recurrent depression with chronic suicidal thoughts. Despite numerous medications and long-term outpatient therapy, Bethany remained depressed. She had had a normal childhood until her parents divorced and her father moved to another city. After that, the family's finances changed. Bethany was moved from a private school where she had done quite well to a public school where she felt bored and less "special." Her mother was no longer able to afford the singing lessons that Bethany had loved so much.

Other than these events, there were no other significant traumas in her life.

During one of our sessions, I asked Bethany to draw three pictures: one to depict her emotions at the time of her parent's divorce, another when her eating disorder started at age fourteen, and the final one to demonstrate her current emotions.

The first picture was a scrawl of bright red crayon covering the entire page that screamed "I am ANGRY!" The second picture showed the bright red scrawls being covered up with dark purple, which she interpreted as her attempt to cover up the anger that had never gone away or been acknowledged. The final picture showed the bright red scrawls again covered over with dark purple and on top of this, black was painted over the purple and the red, demonstrating the dark oblivion of her depression and the final attempt to suppress her anger.

Bethany was surprised that she felt anger at all, so complete was the cover-up. By unveiling her anger, she opened the door to a deeper possibility of healing.

Bethany demonstrates the primeval emotional soup that many of our patients swim in when feelings suppressed in childhood get obscured over many years into adulthood so that they become very difficult to recognize.

Sensate Level

Beneath this emotional soup is the sensate level of emotions that are felt and sometimes trapped in our bodies. This concept is central to effectiveness of many of the CAM body therapies that we will discuss and can often be understood in terms of metaphors: shoulder spasm from the stress of working too much can be described as "carrying the weight of the world on your shoulders." Uncovering the many layers of the emotional soup and their attendant physical manifestations allows one to uncover deeply held beliefs that are blocks to the self-healing process.

Because patients with eating disorders are disconnected from their physical bodies, they do not receive any of the cues that would force them to eat or stop eating in response to hunger and satiety or to stop exercising before they injure their bodies. Their complete attention is focused on their eating disorder thoughts, those negative, self-defeating thoughts that bombard their waking minutes, seeking always to destroy the individual.

Therefore, one key to healing body, mind, and spirit is to reconnect with the body and to remember how to experience emotions in the body. What does anger feel like? Is anger signaled by a flush of heat and reddening of the face? Does anger feel like tightness in the shoulders or chest? How does fear feel? Or anxiety? Or shame? Little by little, it is important to be able to recognize the sensations from the body and to understand that they are cues to our innermost feelings, feelings that have been submerged through the use of food, drugs, drinking, or compulsive sex. The sensations in the body are the key to unlocking the emotions and removing oneself from the primeval emotional soup.

Core Beliefs

Core beliefs lie beneath the emotional soup and sensate level and are the pivotal points on which the eating disorder and addictions have been honed. Getting at these core beliefs can be difficult, although once recognized, they form a "light bulb" moment that can transform one's attachment to and understanding of the origins of an eating disorder.

George presented for treatment at the age of forty-three. He was married with two young sons and worked in his own business in Detroit, Michigan. George was a compulsive overeater who at six-foot-three weighed close to four hundred pounds. He had struggled with his weight since childhood. In treatment, he was able to get in touch with a great deal of anger toward his mother. As a young child, he had been sickly and his mother was overprotective. When he and his brothers got into trouble, they got punished and he did not. Over time, this led to his being teased by his older brother. At about the age of fourteen, he was taller and was heavier than his brother John. During one of their many fights, George became so enraged that he literally broke down John's bedroom door. In an instant, he realized that John was actually afraid of him and his rage for the first time ever. George remembers having the thought in that instant: "big is good."

This became his long-forgotten core belief that would sabotage future efforts to lose weight. Being big was his protection and his power. Being big was the equalizer between his tormentor and himself. The need to "be big" to have power also became generalized to other stressful situations. For example, in his marriage, where his wife's financial prowess gave her an advantage in the power differential of their marriage, being big helped to ease some of the loss of self-esteem he felt not being the primary breadwinner.

Core beliefs represent essential human needs: the need for love, nurturing or acceptance. Core beliefs are the result of chronic stressors that remain unresolved or of extreme emotions. As such, they remain very deeply in memory. These beliefs then shape future behaviors but surreptitiously are unremembered. Therefore, the behaviors would appear to contradict one's stated goals. For example, George wanted to lose weight and he was often successful in doing so, but inevitably the weight would return and very quickly. Armed with an understanding of at least one of the core beliefs that would sabotage his weight loss, he was more aware and more able to intervene and change this belief. For his child-self, big was good. As an adult, being big or obese was killing him. He had developed high cholesterol and insulin resistance as well as high blood pressure. He was often easily fatigued and unable to play with his children in the way he would have liked. "Big" had helped him deal with a childhood in which he was teased and felt afraid of his older brother, but it was no longer an asset; instead, it was a liability.

Deeper Urges of the Soul

One does not have to believe in religion or even have a belief in a "higher power" to understand and acknowledge the deeper urges of the soul or spirit. These urges are sometimes called our "bliss" or passion in life. Most importantly, the deeper urges are our own unique, individual method of self-expression. Self-expression is hampered when our focus, thoughts, and energy are 100 percent occupied with eating disorder thinking.

While one may continue attempting to go to school or maintain a successful career or be an ideal mother, the deck will be stacked against being successful or experiencing happiness while doing these things he or she may treasure because of the elaborate structure required for emotion control. Often, when restored to a more complete way of functioning, these persons may realize that what they considered their best performance at work, for example, didn't come close to what they are able to do when well. There is no way for persons under the influence of an eating disorder to get in touch with these spiritual longings until they move through and clear out the layers of their elaborate structure – the superficial behaviors and emotional soup—then get back in touch with their bodies through the sensations and core beliefs layers. Once this is accomplished, the stirrings of their spirit/soul begin to percolate to the surface, bringing along a renewed vigor for and purpose in life.

CHAPTER 2
YOU CAN NEVER BE TOO THIN

"If you want to become full, let yourself be empty.
"If you want to be reborn, let yourself die."
Lao-tzu, *Tao Te Ching*

A desire for thinness is often the common ground for all eating disorders, fueling the multibillion-dollar diet industry. This chapter provides basic information about the full spectrum of eating disorders from anorexia to compulsive overeating, the DSM diagnostic criteria, prevalence, and prognoses. The questions of what integrative medicine is and what it contributes to the treatment of eating disorders are explored.

O ver seven million girls and women and one million boys and men will suffer from an eating disorder in their lifetimes. Up to 3.7 percent of females will be diagnosed with anorexia nervosa and an estimated 4.2 percent will have bulimia nervosa. An additional 2 to 5 percent will fall into the newest eating disorder category under consideration: binge eating disorder. Nineteen percent of college-age females are bulimic; many go undiagnosed until much later. Up to one quarter of anorexics will die prematurely as a result of their disease. At the other end of the spectrum, 2 to 5 percent of the population falls into the category of binge eating disorder (B.E.D.). In the United States, food and weight are significant issues; almost half of the population is considered overweight and/or obese.

Eating disorders begin early, with 10 percent of patients diagnosed when they are younger than ten years of age. One-third of patients are diagnosed in preteens and adolescents up to age fifteen. In total, 86 percent of patients are diagnosed with eating disorders before the age of twenty.

Earlier studies suggested disparities in the occurrence of eating disorders among different ethnic groups. Current research demonstrates that eating disorder symptoms may be as common or more common among certain ethnic groups (Asians, blacks, and Hispanics) compared with Caucasians.[6] There was also no difference found in dieting and restraint scores among Asian, Latino, and white adolescent girls and boys [7] and no difference in binge behavior or B.E.D. in obese patients who sought to lose weight with bariatric surgery.[8] These changes may be related to an extension of cultural or media ideals of what is attractive or may represent underreporting in the past. However, an analysis of eighteen studies from 1987-2001 concluded that African-American women were less likely than white women to have an eating disorder.[9] As well, a study in school-age girls demonstrated that Native American girls had higher rates of restricting/purging and dieting than whites or nonwhite/non-Native American populations.[10]

Genetics and Eating Disorders

Newer genetic studies have shown evidence of a contribution of genetic factors to the incidence of eating disorders. These studies are based on twin studies in various populations. They demonstrate an interesting phenomenon—that genetic factors may be more important at some stages in the development of an eating disorder (ED) and less important in later stages. These factors need to be studied across the life span to accurately account for their contribution. An individual's psychological makeup can contribute to the development of an eating disorder. Perfectionistic or obsessional personality traits are important contributors to the development of restrictive anorexia. For bulimics, traits such as low self-esteem, ineffectiveness, poor self confidence, and feelings of personal inadequacy may be contributing factors. It is most likely that a genetic predisposition and vulnerability combined with adverse conditions such as extreme dieting or emotional stress are responsible for the development of eating disorders.[11] Although genetics are interesting to study, people cannot change their genetic makeup. Therefore, the applicability of current genetic studies to eating disorders is related to their potential in identifying those at high risk and providing preventive education strategies to this group.

Eating disorders have one of the highest death rates of all psychiatric diagnoses. The number of deaths in anorexics is 11.6 times what would be expected in people of the same age and sex; for bulimics, this number is 1.3 times. The most shocking number is the 56.9 times difference in the number of observed versus expected deaths in anorexics from suicide. If either of these groups abuses alcohol, the death rates are even higher.[12] Depression is a major risk factor for both substance use disorder and bulimia and explains to a great degree the association between substance use disorder and bulimia.[13] A meta-analysis of forty-two studies of mortality in eating disorder patients found 178 deaths in 3,006 patients: 54 percent from complications of their disease, 27 percent from suicide, and 19 percent from other or unknown causes. The mortality rate was estimated in this study to be 0.56 percent per year and was 12 times greater than the expected death rate for women between fifteen and twenty-four; the suicide rate is 75 times greater.[14] Suicide attempts occur in both anorexics and bulimics, and the unique predictors for anorexics include severity of depression and drug use; for bulimics, a history of drug use and the use of laxatives significantly increased the risk for suicide attempts.[15]

Another factor influencing the development of eating disorders is acculturation. Studies show that young women from south Asia, Egypt, Pakistan, and Greece have a higher risk for the development of eating disorders. In general, the incidence is higher in those who are exposed to Western culture, images, and ideals of beauty.

In the past, eating disorders were considered discrete entities with little or no commonality. Now, eating disorders are thought to be part of a spectrum from anorexia at one end to compulsive overeaters and binge eaters at the other end. Many eating disorder patients start at one end of the spectrum and end up at the other. What are the similarities and differences? From psychiatry's viewpoint, specific criteria need to be present to make the diagnosis of an eating disorder:

DSM-IV definition 1996 (Diagnostic and Statistical Manual)[1]

Anorexia Nervosa
May be restricting type or binge-eating/purging type
1. Refusal to maintain body weight at or above a minimally normal weight for age and height (e.g. weight reduction less than 85% of expected or failure to gain weight during growth to less than 85% of expected)
2. Unrealistic fear of gaining weight or becoming fat
3. Unrealistic appraisal of body weight or shape or denial of seriousness of current low body weight.
4. In postmenarcheal females, amenorrhea (i.e. absence of at least 3 consecutive menstrual cycles.)

---

[1] *Reprinted with permission from the Diagnostic and Statistical Manual of Mental Disorders, Fourth Edition, Text Revision, (Copyright 2000). American Psychiatric Association.*

Common Co-Morbidities:
Obsessive-compulsive disorder
Personality disorders
Major depressive disorder
Social phobia
Body dysmorphic disorder
Substance use disorders
Medical complications

Bulimia Nervosa

Note: may be purging type (self-induced vomiting or using laxatives) or nonpurging type (exercise or fasting)

1. Inappropriate behavior to compensate for overeating (e.g. self-induced vomiting, laxatives, diuretics, fasting)
2. Binge eating and compensation at least twice a week for 3 months
3. Self-evaluation is unduly influenced by body shape and weight
4. Not due to anorexia.
5. Recurrent episodes of binge eating
   a. Eating, in a discrete period of time (e.g. up to two hours) an amount of food that is definitely larger than most people would eat during a similar period of time and under similar circumstances.
   b. A sense of lack of control during the episode

Common Co-Morbidities:
Major depressive disorder
Dysthymic Disorder
Social phobia
Anxiety disorders
Medical complications

Binge eating disorder/Compulsive Eating (listed as a disorder meriting further study in DSM-IV)

1. Recurrent episodes of binge eating. An episode is characterized by:

     a. Eating a larger amount of food than normal during a short period of time (within any two hour period)

2. Lack of control over eating during the binge episode (i.e. the feeling that one cannot stop eating).
   a. Binge eating episodes are associated with three or more of the following:.
   b. Eating until feeling uncomfortably full Eating large amounts of food when not physically hungry
   c. Eating much more rapidly than normal
   d. Eating alone because you are embarrassed by how much you're eating
   e. Feeling disgusted, depressed, or guilty after overeating
3. Marked distress regarding binge eating is present
4. Binge eating occurs, on average, at least 2 days a week for six months
5. The binge eating is not associated with the regular use of inappropriate compensatory behavior (i.e. purging, excessive exercise, etc.) and does not occur exclusively during the course of bulimia nervosa or anorexia nervosa

Common Co-Morbidities:

Major depressive disorders

Anxiety disorders/panic

Personality disorders

Note: Binge Eating and Compulsive Eating are frequently used interchangeably, generally describing a pattern of overeating as a coping mechanism for emotional pain. Some experts consider these as two separate entities with compulsive eating relating to a condition that includes overeating consistently without 'binges' and Binge Eating Disorder relating to a pattern of normal eating interspersed with episodes of bingeing.

Eating Disorder – Not Otherwise Specified (ED-NOS)
1. All criteria for Anorexia Nervosa are met **except that,**

in females, regular periods are present.

2. All criteria for Bulimia Nervosa are met **except that bingeing and consequent inappropriate compensatory behaviours occur less than twice a week or for a duration of less than 3 months**.

3. Regular use of inappropriate compensatory behaviour (such as vomiting) by individuals of a normal body weight after eating small amount of food. *(An individual of low body weight (or reaching a low body weight after being diagnosed with an ED-NOS) might well be considered anorexic, or bulimic if "bingeing" occurred as defined by the diagnostic criteria).*

4. Repeatedly chewing and spitting out (but not consuming) large amounts of food.

5. Recurrent episodes of binge eating in the absence of the regular use of inappropriate compensatory behaviours characteristic of bulimia nervosa. *(Binge Eating Disorders/Compulsive Eating).*

Only through individual patient stories, however, does one begin to get a feel for what lies beneath the behaviors or symptoms required to make an eating disorder diagnosis. Only through hearing these stories can one understand the compulsions, beliefs, thought patterns, and desperate attempts by patients to distance themselves from their emotional pain that is the driving force that sustains the eating disorder.

There are many theories as to what contributes to the incidence of eating disorders in the population. Brumberg,[16] Miller,[17] and others[18] reported that books and magazines touting calorie counting, the fashion industry promoting slimness, TV and movies promoting being thin as the way to be sexy and successful, and the current emphasis on fitness and athleticism all contribute to the increasing incidence of eating disorders. Changes in cultural norms have also been cited. Previous generations' norms of beauty idealized a figure with curves, a la Marilyn Monroe. The icons for women today are much thinner, some even emaciated. This change in the body shape and size our culture sees as beautiful may explain the increase in eating disorders since the 1960s. There are many other theories to explain the reason why anorexia develops:

1. Anorexia can be described as the extension of determined dieting. All EDs have in common the desire to control weight and appearance.

2. Anorectic families are described as enmeshed, vacillating between overprotectiveness and abandonment. Minuchin[19] noted that the maintenance of the symptomatic child often defused parental conflicts, thereby keeping the family in "balance."

3. The viewpoint of cognitive behavioral therapy advocates is that anorexia is a learned behavior maintained by positive reinforcement. The individual diets to lose weight and is reinforced by peers and society. Reinforcement for weight loss is so powerful that the individual maintains the anorexic behavior despite threats to health and well-being.

4. Some view anorexia as an attempt of the self to refuse itself with a dissolution of the link between the self and the body. When negative expectations occur that anorexics are not able to meet, they rise above the need to a place of superiority over the need, i.e., a place of "not needing."[20]

5. Family theories view eating disorders as a cry for help of a conflicted and dysfunctional family.

There are also internal psychological factors that contribute to the development of any eating disorder, such as low self-esteem, lack of control in one's life, loneliness, anger, depression, or anxiety. Relationships within the family of origin are key to understanding the development of eating disorders as well as interpersonal relationships outside the family. Difficulty expressing emotions or a history of being teased for being overweight or in some way being ridiculed about one's appearance can also be contributing factors. More studies now confirm the link between any type of trauma—

neglect, emotional, physical, or sexual abuse—to the development of an eating disorder.

Current treatment strategies do not address the needs of many ED patients, and few have been associated with proven long-term success. The most rigorous review on the treatment of bulimia nervosa (BN) is the one done by the National Institute for Clinical Excellence (NICE), an organization in England and Wales that develops evidence-based guidelines for treatment of BN. The NICE review reached three conclusions:

1. The most effective form of therapy for BN is a specialized type of cognitive behavioral therapy (CBT-BN) that involves sixteen to twenty individual sessions over a short time period (five months). Early behavior change was the best predictor of long-term success with CBT-BN. CBT-BN still results in only 50 percent of patients experiencing full recovery, highlighting the need for investigating other therapies.

2. The alternative therapy studied - interpersonal psychotherapy—has the same amount of total time with the therapist but over a longer time frame. Improvements in ED symptoms using interpersonal psychotherapy took eight to twelve months longer than CBT-BN. The effectiveness of group versus individual therapy is still not clear from the available research.

3. Neither antidepressant drugs or some self-help programs (with or without professional therapy) demonstrated full or lasting results and therefore should be viewed as possible first steps. If antidepressants are used for BN, fluoxetine (Prozac) is the drug of choice at a dose of 60 mg per day.[21]

Studies on the treatment of anorexia nervosa (AN) have been hampered by high drop-out rate and anorectics' lack of desire to give up their illness. The NICE report found few randomized controlled trials (RCTs). Its recommendations included:

1. Outpatient management should be handled by experienced professionals.

2. When necessary, inpatient treatment should be in a closely monitored setting.
3. Treatment of children and adolescent anorectics should include family therapy.

These recommendations are based on minimal research evidence but agree with the American Psychiatric Association Workgroup 2000.[22] The Royal Australian and New Zealand College of Psychiatrists (2004) offered an alternative set of recommendations based on expert opinion and not on controlled trials. The recommendations included a multidimensional approach to AN with close medical supervision and return to a normal weight. There were no specific psychotherapeutic recommendations except for family therapy as above. The psychiatrists also recommended treatment of comorbid depression.[23]

The Cochrane Review included six small studies on outpatients and concluded that no specific type of psychotherapeutic approach was better than another. Dietary advice alone resulted in high drop-out rates, and "treatment as usual" performed very poorly. It was concluded that there was an urgent need for larger, better designed studies.[24]

The difficulty in treating AN and BN is mirrored in the lack of effective treatment for binge eating disorder and compulsive overeating. A review of studies that examined the effectiveness of prescription antiobesity agents—orlistat and sibutramine—showed both drugs to be moderately effective in promoting weight loss. However, these study results were hampered by the high drop-out rate of participants.[25] A long-term study of sixty-eight patients with BED whose mean age was 29.3 years showed 57.4 percent had a good outcome (based on a global score that included self-reports, professional assessments, eating disorder symptoms, and psychological pathology measures), 35.3 percent had an intermediate outcome, 5.9 percent had poor outcomes, and one person died. In this study, the patients showed substantial improvement while in treatment with a decline over the next three years and stabilization and improvement in years four, five, and six.[26]

In the past decade, bariatric surgery has become an option for the treatment of obesity. A review of studies on the safety and efficacy of weight loss surgery showed that patients who chose this option lost more weight and had improvement in their quality of life. The risks included complications such as wound infection, side effects such as heartburn, and the risk of death. Gastric bypass surgery resulted in the loss of more weight and was less likely to require repeat surgery than vertical-banded gastroplasty. Weight loss was similar among those having laparoscopic versus open surgery, but there were fewer complications with laparoscopic surgery. The quality of most of the studies was poor and so it is difficult to draw any conclusions about which procedure is best.[27]

A review of thirty-six studies including over three thousand patients on the efficacy of cognitive behavioral therapy, behavioral modification therapy, hypnotherapy, and relaxation therapy found that behavior therapy alone resulted in more weight lost than a placebo treatment. When combined with diet and exercise, behavior therapy or cognitive behavior therapy versus diet and exercise alone, the combined therapy resulted in greater weight reduction. There was not enough evidence to evaluate hypnotherapy or relaxation therapy, but the available evidence suggests that these therapies may also be beneficial in weight loss.

Finally, although there are few head-to-head comparisons of different diets, current evidence shows that energy-restricted dieting does not result in sustained weight loss over twelve to eighteen months. Low-fat diets were not found to be any better than other types of diets for long-term weight loss/maintenance.[28]

The majority of patients who are overweight or obese have tried and failed numerous diets. To date, research studies cannot determine if any one particular diet is more effective than another. The only diet with extensive research to support its efficacy is the Ornish diet. It has been studied mainly in terms of its ability to lower cardiovascular risk, although for those who are able to stay on the diet, there is usually substantial weight loss.

The lack of specific and long-lasting therapies to treat

eating disorders means that more research is needed into other types of treatments. An integrative medicine approach to the treatment of eating disorders includes eight cornerstones as shown below. Psychotherapy and the use of psychopharmacology are well covered in other excellent books. The discussion below will focus on those parts of this approach that are unique.

8 Cornerstones of an Integrative Approach to ED

☐ **Nutrition Program** ▫ Shift the patient's relationship with food ▫ Improve the patient's **autonomy in relationship to food** ▫ Search for Root causes of dysfunction around food ▫ Improve digestion and absorption	☐ **Psychotherapy** ▫ Insight ▫ Food/mood ▫ **Body image** ▫ Root cause ▫ Family Therapy
☐ **Exercise** ▫ Learn healthy behaviors ▫ Get in touch with physical body ▫ **Learn body cues**	☐ **Nutraceuticals** ▫ **Support medication effects** ▫ Decrease side effects ▫ **Address specific nutritional deficiencies in ED**
☐ **Psychometrics** ▫ Early identification of Axis I and II diagnoses ▫ Inform treatment approaches ▫ **Pre- and Posttesting**	☐ **Skills training** ▫ Emotional regulation ▫ Practical skills ▫ Distress Tolerance ▫ Integration of insights
☐ **Pharmaceuticals** ▫ Used when necessary ▫ Stabilization of patients	☐ **Complementary and Alternative Therapies** ▫ Mind-Body Medicine ▫ Acupuncture ▫ Chiropractic ▫ Energy Medicine ▫ Massage ▫ Shiatsu

Integrative medicine is defined as a "healing-oriented discipline that takes into account the whole person—body, mind, and spirit—including all aspects of lifestyle. It *emphasizes the therapeutic relationship and makes use of both conventional and alternative therapies."* [*]

Eating disorders comprise a group of conditions that are difficult to treat and have high morbidity and mortality. Conventional approaches combined with complementary and alternative therapies offer additive benefits not found with either alone.

---

[*] Definition developed by the Program in Integrative Medicine, University of Arizona, Tucson, AZ. Dr. Andrew Weil, director

CHAPTER 3
CORNERSTONES – FOOD IS MEDICINE

"One-quarter of what you eat keeps you alive. The other three-quarters keeps your doctor alive."
(Hieroglyph found in an ancient Egyptian tomb)

"The doctor of the future will no longer treat the human frame with drugs, but rather will cure and prevent disease with nutrition."
Thomas Edison

This chapter explores how the building blocks of nutrition affect mood and health and offers research demonstrating that changing nutritional status alone can affect disordered eating behaviors. This chapter also discusses dietary supplements: vitamins, minerals, and herbal products used to replace missing nutrients, support effects of psychopharmacological therapy, and remove barriers to refeeding.

T he ancient physician Hippocrates (460-359 B.C.) said, "Let thy food be thy medicine, and let thy medicine be thy food." While this may be the earliest statement extolling the necessity of nutrition for good health, it certainly was not the last.

In the early development of scientific Western medicine, there was a turning away from these basic principles of the importance of nutrition in health as pharmaceutical therapies took center stage in the treatment armamentarium.

Starving for Science

The importance of nutrition is nowhere so pronounced as in the case of eating disorders. While many may think that undernutrition or malnutrition is a side effect of an eating disorder, studies have documented that it can be the cause of many eating disorder symptoms. The earliest study to demonstrate this was done by Ancel Keys[29] and his colleagues at the University of Minnesota in 1950. Young, healthy, psychologically normal males were recruited for the study as an alternative to military service. Of the hundred who applied, thirty-six were selected as being in the best physical and psychological health. This study is known as the "starvation study" and its intent was not to study eating disorders, but for the development of a better understanding of how best to manage the refeeding of concentration camp survivors.

In the study the men ate normally and continued their normal activities for the first three months while their behavior, personality, and eating patterns were studied. Over the next six months, their diet was restricted to half of what they normally ate, resulting in a 25 percent weight loss. Note that the number of calories prescribed in the study is the same as that now in treating obesity. After this period of weight loss, the men were slowly restored to their previous caloric intake. The results of the study included only thirty-two of the original thirty-six; four dropped out either during or at the end of the "semistarvation" phase. All participants experienced very dramatic physical, psychological, and social changes.

The striking changes during the starvation period included an increase in preoccupation with food. The volunteers toyed with their food; they often made what might be considered weird or disgusting food concoctions, developed food rituals, and hoarded food. Their preoccupation with food included a spectrum of behaviors including collecting recipes (an activity in which they had no interest before beginning the study); others changed their careers (including three who became chefs and one who went into agriculture). Coffee and tea consumption increased excessively and the volunteers also engaged in excessive gum chewing (up to forty packs a day) during the starvation phase of the study. Several of the men were unable to tolerate their hunger and engaged in binge eating, followed by self-criticism and guilt.

During the twelve week refeeding period, bingeing continued and several of the men experienced nausea and vomiting. Serious binge eating occurred in a subset of volunteers. Binges consisted of up to ten thousand calories, with volunteers reporting continued hunger even after bingeing to the point of becoming ill. Normalization of eating behaviors took approximately five months for the majority of the volunteers.

The volunteers also experienced emotional changes including depression, which worsened during the course of the experiment. Some participants also experienced extreme mood swings. Other changes included irritability, anxiety, and apathy. Some neglected personal hygiene. Two developed psychosis. These changes persisted for some time during the refeeding period. The men became increasingly isolated during the semistarvation period and reported decreased sex drive, which took almost eight months to be restored to the previous level of functioning.

The volunteers also experienced decreased concentration and other cognitive changes as well as physical changes that included decreased need for sleep, gastrointestinal problems, dizziness, headaches, noise and light sensitivity, weakness, fluid retention, cold intolerance, and difficulties with hearing and sight. There was a 40 percent slowing of basal metabolic rate, lower body temperature, and decreases in heart rate and respiration. Metabolic rates increased during refeeding and were proportional to number of calories consumed.

Why is this study so important? One of the legacies of this experiment is the understanding that starvation has a dramatic effect on personality and that nutrition directly affects the mind as well as the body. The study also demonstrated to the scientific community the mutability of the human body, i.e., that diet alone can affect body functions such as blood pressure, cholesterol, and resting heart rate. These functions were previously thought to be relatively fixed. The study is also cited by those who study the effect of food deprivation on the cognitive and social functioning of those with eating disorders[30]. Many of the symptoms seen in anorexia and bulimia were present in the starvation study and, given that the volunteers were psychologically healthy, could not be blamed on pre-existing psychological problems. These symptoms affected all aspects of the volunteers' lives—physical, social, and psychological. This study also demonstrated the body's amazing capacity to survive. During semistarvation, all of the body's focus is on ensuring the survival of the species and other activities— including social or sexual functions— are secondary to the focus on food.

At the end of this study, despite the high caloric intake of the volunteers during refeeding, none became obese. There was an average of 10 percent increase in weight over their prestudy weight. The increase was lost in the six months after completion of the study.

This study helps those suffering with eating disorders to understand that their symptoms are not "all in their head." The study is also a powerful demonstration of Hippocrates's maxim of food as medicine.

There are other studies in modern research that demonstrate the importance of nutrition and its effect on symptoms of disordered eating. For example, a study done on women with either BN or binge eating disorder (BED) showed that a protein supplement given three hours before a meal reduced binge eating while a carbohydrate supplement did not. Participants also consumed less food at meals and were less hungry after receiving the protein supplementation.[31] A small study by Dalvit-McPhillips[32] in the 1980s showed that if bulimic women were given a "nutrient-dense" diet (one without blood sugar destabilizers such as white flour, refined sugar, alcohol, caffeine, flavor enhancers, and decreased salt), their bingeing behavior stopped. This type of diet may today be consistent with a diet without foods that have low glycemic index. Participants were also given vitamin C, a B-complex vitamin, and a multivitamin. Those on the nutrient-dense diet ceased bingeing and were able to lose weight effortlessly and remained binge-free for two and a half years. When the control group was put on the nutrient-dense diet, participants also stopped bingeing. This study suggests that malnutrition and blood sugar insulin level are important factors in the bingeing behavior of bulimics.

In summary, with the starvation diet, a diet very similar to that of many eating disorder patients, Keys demonstrated very dramatically the connection between diet, mood disorders, preoccupation with food, and other symptoms that are present in varying severity in ED patients. Other studies show that there are specific nutrients that are missing or lacking in patients with eating disorders. Biochemical research and population studies have shown that specific vitamins and mineral deficiencies are associated with symptoms such as mood disorders, cognitive dysfunction, and other symptoms found in eating disorder patients. Case reports and small studies that compare the effects of dietary changes such as protein supplementation between meals or the use of the nutrient-dense diet further demonstrate that in ED patients, these affect behaviors such as bingeing and purging. While different studies address the different ED diagnoses—some studies were done only with anorexics or only with bulimics—there is no reason to doubt that B vitamins have the same or similar functions in an anorexic or binge eater as in a bulimic. The severity of symptoms varies with the severity of the deficiency or the degree of malnutrition.

A supplement program therefore must address: 1) nutrient deficiencies shown in eating disorder patients, 2) preventive nutritional needs to address conditions for which ED patients are at higher risk (e.g., osteoporosis), and 3) treatment of symptoms with known connections to nutritional deficits (e.g., depression, anxiety, and gastrointestinal symptoms). The following nutraceutical program addresses all three by offering: 1) biochemical function of the specific nutrient, 2) food sources of the nutrient, 3) dosages and side effects/interactions with medications, and 4) research evidence to support its use in ED patients or in the treatment of symptoms found in ED patients.

Nutraceuticals are defined as vitamins, minerals, and dietary supplements used for therapeutic purposes. Vitamin and mineral deficiencies can also contribute to symptoms seen in eating disorder patients.

B Vitamins

The B vitamins are vital to human nutrition because of their role in transporting oxygen to the brain and providing protection from harmful free radicals. B vitamins also convert glucose, which our food is broken down into, into energy in the brain cells and assist in the manufacture of neurotransmitters. B_{12} is essential for nerve cell health. Studies in animals document that a deficiency can slow the rate at which rats learn, and studies in older people with deficiencies of this vitamin show that it can be the cause of mental deterioration and confusion. Folic acid deficiency can cause macrocytic anemia, a condition in which the red blood cells grow bigger to carry more oxygen when there are fewer cells available for this task. There are no known harmful effects when taken in the recommended doses. Niacin at doses over 50 milligrams can cause the skin to flush.[33] Vitamin B_{12} and folic acid have significant mood-enhancing benefits when used alone and in combination with antidepressants.

> B_{12} is found in eggs, meat, poultry, shellfish, and milk products. Folate (B_9) is found mainly in beans and legumes, citrus fruits, whole grains, dark leafy vegetables, poultry, pork, shellfish, and liver. Standard dose of B_{12} is 10-1,000 mcg/day; folic acid, 400-800 mcg/day.

Low B_{12} and low folic acid levels have been noted in patients with depression. In addition, population studies have found an association between depression and low levels of these two vitamins. ED patients with depression may suffer from malnutrition-induced depression in much the same way that drug or alcohol use can cause mood disorders. The lack of nutrients could contribute to depression in ED patients. Increased homocysteine is also a marker for low folate and vitamin B_{12} levels, and patients with depression have been found to have high levels of homocysteine. Depressed patients in a large population study done in Norway were found to have an increase in homocysteine levels. Low folate levels have been associated with depression in alcoholic patients. Low levels of folate have also been implicated in poor response rates to standard antidepressant therapy.[34] A search of randomized controlled research studies on the effectiveness of folate for depression found that folate enhanced the effectiveness of antidepressants in the treatment of depression significantly but was not found to be effective when used alone.[35] Other studies have found that oral supplementation with the co-enzyme form of folic acid at doses of 15-50 mg daily was effective in improving symptoms of depression.[36]

Lake[37] reported doses of folate from 800 mcg (80 mg) up to 5 mg and B_{12} of 1 mg/day to improve mood and energy when used alone. This combination of B_{12} and folic acid may also enhance the efficacy of alternative treatments for depression such as SAMe (discussed later in this chapter).

Several small studies have shown deficiencies in other B vitamins in patients with eating disorders: niacin (B_3), pyridoxine (B_6), and thiamine (B_1). Of note is that the first symptom of niacin deficiency is anorexia (the medical term for "loss of appetite"). There is some thought that anorexia nervosa may be a subclinical form of *pellagra*, of which edema is often a symptom. Niacin supplementation has been shown in several cases to improve appetite and mental status. Pyridoxine plays a role in balancing hormones.

Zinc and Other Micronutrients

Other micronutrients have been shown to be missing in eating disorder patients. Symptoms of zinc deficiency include a decrease in smell and taste, loss of appetite, mental lethargy, generalized hair loss, diarrhea, rough and dry skin, slow wound healing, and delayed puberty.

> **Food sources and dosages of zinc and copper**: Zinc can be found in oysters, herring, pumpkin seeds, sunflower seeds, seafood, meats, mushrooms, soybeans, eggs, figs, avocados, and cantaloupe. Copper is found in organ meats, seafood, nuts, legumes, blackstrap molasses, and raisins. Taking more than 40 mg/day (for adults) of zinc may decrease copper absorption and result in anemia. Elemental zinc as high as 80 mg/day can be used safely when given with copper 2 mg. The RDA for zinc is 8 mg/day for women and 11mg/day for men.

Zinc is important for a variety of reasons and must be kept in balance. Copper, calcium, and phosphorus all increase the effectiveness of zinc. Zinc is also vital in the metabolism of essential fatty acids (EFAs); EFAs are likewise important in the absorption of zinc. Zinc is a cofactor in the absorption of the B vitamins[38] as is manganese and magnesium. Zinc is vital in the regulation of gene expression, immune function, wound healing, reproduction, growth and development, behavior and learning, blood clotting, thyroid hormone function, and insulin action. Zinc therefore plays a role in maintenance of stable blood sugar, and people with hypoglycemia may be deficient in zinc.

One double-blind, placebo-controlled study demonstrated that zinc was superior to placebo in reducing hyperactive, impulsive, and impaired socialization symptoms in patients with ADHD (attention deficit hyperactivity disorder) but not helpful in reducing attention deficit symptoms. ADHD is one of the comorbid disorders prevalent in eating disorders.[39] In a study of adolescent anorexics, zinc deficiency was diagnosed as secondary to not eating enough foods containing zinc. When zinc was supplemented (50 mg elemental zinc/day), there was a decrease in depression and anxiety levels as measured on the Zung Depression Scale and the State-Trait Anxiety Inventory.[40] Zinc supplementation (100 mg of zinc gluconate) has been shown to help with weight gain in anorexics, increasing their body mass index BMI) twice as fast as placebo.[41] Zinc also lowers the severity and duration of diarrhea associated with malnutrition.

> **Food sources of omega-3 fatty acids** include oily fish; flaxseeds; certain oils including canola oil, fish oil, flaxseed oil, soybean oil, and walnut oil; walnuts; and pumpkin seeds.

Omega-3 Fatty Acids

Omega-3 and omega-6 fatty acids are essential fatty acids (EFAs) because they cannot be synthesized by the body and must be obtained through diet or supplementation. The types of omega-3 fatty acids include: eicosapentaenoic acid (EPA) and docosahexaenoic acid (DHA), found in fish and fish oils, and alpha-linoleic acid (ALA), which is found in seeds and oils, green leafy vegetables, walnuts, and soybeans. ALA is converted through an inefficient enzymatic process to EPA and DHA. Both are precursors to a group of *eicosanoids* that are precursors to prostaglandins, thromboxanes, and leukotrienes that are anti-inflammatory, antithrombotic, antiarrhythmic, and vasodilatory. Omega-3 FAs are important in brain cell communication, therefore having significant effects on brain function and mood. Omega-6 FAs such as linoleic acid (LA) are present in grains, meats, and the seeds of most plants. LA is precursor to a different group of *eicosanoids*, including arachidonic acid, that tends to promote inflammation and blood clot formation.

The diet of early humans supplied a ratio of 1:1 omega-6 to omega-3 FAs. The modern American diet is approximately 10:1. This change may be seen as tipping the balance toward diseases related to the proinflammatory and thrombotic (clot-forming) effects of Omega-6 FAs.

Omega-3 versus Omega-6 Oils:
Omega-3: canola, fish, flaxseed, soybean, and walnut oil
Omega-6: borage, corn, cottonseed, grape seed, peanut, primrose, safflower, sesame, soybean, and sunflower oils

---

Omega-3 fatty acids offer several benefits in the treatment of eating disorders.

In the Overweight or Obese Patient:

Consumption of omega-3 FAs has a beneficial effect on insulin sensitivity and glucose tolerance as well as useful benefits for eating disorder patients who are obese or diagnosed with metabolic syndrome (central obesity, impaired glucose tolerance, hypertension, and abnormal levels of cholesterol and other lipids in the blood (dyslipidemia).[42]

Omega-3 FAs have been shown to lower serum triglyceride levels, especially in those with high triglycerides, such as diabetics. Consumption of 4 grams per day of omega-3 fatty acids was shown in a review of human studies to reduce serum triglyceride levels by 25 to 30 percent and to increase low density lipoprotein (LDL) by 5 to 10 percent and HDL by 1 to 3 percent.[43]

Cardioprotective Benefits

Anorexics are at higher risk of sudden death. While there have been no studies specifically addressing the use of omega-

3 FAs in this population, EFAs may provide a significant benefit based on studies on other populations. A prospective, randomized, controlled trial group of over 11,324 patients with known coronary heart disease participated in the GISSI-Prevenzione Trial. The participants were randomized to receive 300 mg of vitamin E, 850 mg of Omega-3 FAs, both, or neither. After three and a half years, the group given omega-3 FAs alone had a 45 to 50 percent reduction in sudden death syndrome caused by abnormal rhythms of the heart (ventricular arrhythmia), and all-cause mortality was reduced by 20 percent. [44]

Mood Disorders
Many studies have shown a benefit of omega-3 FA to treat depression and bipolar disorder. Some epidemiological studies demonstrated that persons who live in countries in which there is high consumption of fish have a lower incidence of depression and bipolar disorder. Several studies have also shown a decrease of omega-3 FA (EPA) levels in patients with depression. In one study, those participants who received supplementation with 1 gram of ethyl-EPA achieved a 50 percent reduction on the Hamilton Depression (HAM-D) Rating Scale score. Taking 1 gram daily was found to be superior to supplementation with either 2 grams or 4 grams per day.[45] Omega-3 fatty acid supplements can be given along with prescription medications for depression and bipolar disorder. In a four-week double-blind study, patients diagnosed with recurrent unipolar depression received either ethyl-EPA or placebo. Highly significant benefits were found with the addition of the ethyl-EPA versus placebo when compared to standard antidepressant medication.[46]

A 1999 Harvard study was performed on thirty bipolar patients with a history of at least one relapse in the prior year. All but eight were on medications. Half of the participants used 9.6 grams of fish oil capsules; the other half received olive oil in addition to usual treatment. The omega-3 FA group stayed in remission significantly longer, with a decrease in depression versus the placebo group. The omega-3 FA supplementation did not decrease their symptoms of mania.[47]

Patients with moderately severe borderline personality disorder (meeting Revised Diagnostic Interview for Borderlines and DSM-IV criteria) treated with 1 gram of ethyleicosapentaenoic acid (E-EPA) had less aggressive behavior and less depression than those on placebo.[48]

Cognitive Function

A study in healthy subjects examined the effect of omega-3 FAs on cognitive and physiological parameters. After omega-3 FA supplementation, the serum ratio of arachidonic acid (proinflammatory) to EPA was markedly reduced. Retesting with the Profile of Mood States (POMS) demonstrated improved mood with reduced anger, anxiety, and depression states and increased vigor in the group taking omega-3 FAs.[49]

The American Heart Association (AHA) recommends eating fish at least twice a week, especially fatty fish that provide EPA and DHA. The AHA also recommends consumption of tofu and other forms of soybeans, canola, walnuts, flaxseed, and their oils containing ALA that can be converted to omega-3 FAs in the body. For those with coronary heart disease, 1 gram of EPA plus DHA per day is recommended. For those who need to lower their triglycerides, 2-4 grams of EPA plus DHA per day should be taken. Dosages range from 1-3 grams for treatment of depression or for prevention of heart disease and up to 9 grams for treatment of bipolar disorder.

Because metabolism of omega-3 FAs can cause oxidative stress, it should be taken with a vitamin E supplement in doses of 400-800 IU daily. Omega-6 FAs (gamma-linoleic acid and linoleic acid) are readily available in the diet in the form of meat, dairy, and vegetable oils, and supplementation is generally not necessary. However, in anorexics with very restrictive diets, omega-6 FA supplementation may be useful. Omega-6 supplements include evening primrose oil, pumpkin oil, borage oil, or hemp oil. Some symptoms of deficiency include hair and nail problems.

Interactions and adverse effects for omega-3 FAs include an increase in bleeding time; however, there are no known cases of abnormal bleeding as a result of omega-3 supplementation, even at high doses or in combination with anticoagulant medications. Fish oil in high doses can increase LDL cholesterol levels, but the clinical significance of this finding is unclear. Side effects include fishy burp or aftertaste and stomach upset. To find out about advisories concerning mercury levels in fish, see: www.epa.gov/waterscience/fish/, www.checnet.org, or www.cfsan.fda.gov/~frf/sea-mehg.html

TABLE: Grams of EPA plus DHA content in an average three-ounce serving of fish:

Herring	
Atlantic	1.71
Pacific	1.81
Salmon	
Chinook	1.48
Atlantic wild	.90 – 1.48
Farmed	1.09 – 1.83
Mackerel	.34 – 1.57
Sardines	.98 – 1.70
Tuna	
Fresh	.24 – 1.28
White, canned in water	.73
Crab, Alaskan king	.35
Flounder/sole	.42
Halibut	.40 – 1.00
Haddock	.20

Calcium

Calcium is important in cellular structure, metabolic function within and between cells, signal transmission, muscle function (including heart function), nerve function, action of enzymes, and normal clotting function. Blood calcium levels are regulated by the hormones calcitonin and parathyroid hormone.

Peak bone mass is related to the development of osteoporosis and risk for fracture later in life. The determinants of peak bone mass include genetic factors, nutrition, and physical activity. Calcium absorption and deposit rates peak in girls before menarche, and calcium intake before puberty may have some effect on the timing of menarche. Some studies indicate that teenage girls are less likely than boys to have adequate intake of calcium in their diets.

This is what research has shown us about calcium:

- Matkovic et al.[50] in a four-year study involving 354 girls at stage 2 puberty found that the mean calcium intake was 830 mg/day. Participants were given an additional 670 mg/day of calcium. Calcium supplementation significantly influenced bone mass during the pubertal growth spurt, an effect that diminished in young adulthood.

- A study by Dodiuk-Gad et al.[51] and a study by Bonjour et al.[52] also demonstrated that calcium supplementation increased bone mineral density at levels that were maintained for three and a half years after the supplements were stopped. In a study of prepubertal children who had <u>high</u> dietary calcium intake, Gibbons et al.[53] did not show an added benefit of calcium supplements on bone, indicating that calcium supplementation may be most beneficial in those whose dietary intake is below normal.

- Calcium supplementation may increase the beneficial effects of physical activity on bone[54].

- Calcium supplements in women at least five years after

menopause who have habitually low calcium intake may reduce bone loss.[55] Furthermore, calcium supplementation of between 500-2,000 mg/day reduces bone loss in postmenopausal women.[56]Supplementation of calcium in the early stages of menopause is not well supported and more research is needed to clarify its importance.

Vitamin D

There is increasing awareness about the importance of vitamin D, not just on bone health but also in relationship to other medical conditions. Vitamin D is important in bone health through its actions on calcium absorption and metabolism. Recent research has shown that vitamin D has a role in reducing risk of cancer, multiple sclerosis, and type 1 (insulin-dependent) diabetes mellitus.

Vitamin D is important to lifelong bone health. Vitamin D status during pregnancy affects the calcium homeostasis of the fetus. In addition, low birth weight in infants appears to be related to vitamin D insufficiency in pregnancy. During youth and adolescence, the role of vitamin D is to optimize bone mineral density. Another role appears to be in reducing risk of multiple sclerosis (MS). Children who received high sun exposure, especially during winter months, had only one-third the risk of developing MS compared with those who had less than one hour of sun exposure daily. Overall, the risk of MS increases rapidly with increasing latitude, a finding that has been demonstrated in Australia, Europe, and the United States. The best explanation for this finding may be that sun exposure and increased vitamin D production in those exposed to the sun during winter helps strengthen the immune system, thereby decreasing the occurrence of viral infections that may give rise to MS. [57 58 59 60 61] There is also evidence that the reduction in the risk of cancer in children may be related to solar UVB exposure/vitamin D. Children in the United Kingdom with a history of frequent childhood sunburns had a reduced risk for prostate cancer. Children and women from Australia were reported to have a risk for non-Hodgkin's lymphoma that was inversely proportional to their history of sun exposure.[62][63]

In adults, low intake of vitamin D and calcium, other dietary factors, and inadequate exercise are the primary risk factors for decreased bone mineral density (BMD). Any medical condition that affects vitamin D absorption—for example, surgical resection of the small intestine where vitamin D is absorbed or inflammatory bowel diseases (IBD) such as Crohn's disease—can increase osteoporosis risk. Corticosteroids that are prescribed for IBD, asthma, skin diseases, and autoimmune diseases (rheumatoid arthritis, lupus, etc.) can reduce absorption of vitamin D and thereby contribute to decreased BMD. Vitamin D is also important in maintaining muscle strength. Research comparing incidence of cancer to maps tracking rate of UVB sun exposure point to a possible role for vitamin D in reducing the risk of seventeen different cancers, with the primary exceptions being cancers related to smoking. Other factors such as urban living, poverty, alcohol consumption, and Hispanic heritage may modify risk of cancers. The influence of vitamin D on cancer risk is supported in research but there have been no double-blind crossover studies of vitamin D supplementation and cancer outcome. The recognition of the correlation between vitamin D and cancer risk is limited in that most studies consider dietary intake of vitamin D rather than including all sources of vitamin D including that obtained through sun exposure. Given this strong evidence, however, it may be wise to consider vitamin D supplementation to be important for good health, not just for its effects on bone. Vitamin D supplementation may be particularly important in the elderly who no longer have as much ability to convert vitamin D in skin through sun exposure and are at higher risk for osteoporosis and falls leading to fractures.Recently, vitamin D has been implicated as an etiological factor in the treatment of persistent nonspecific musculoskeletal pain syndrome. In a study of 150 patients in an outpatient clinic with this diagnosis, 93 percent had deficient vitamin D levels as measured by serum 25-hydroxy vitamin D testing.[64] The risk for vitamin D deficiency was also found to be present in groups usually considered to be at low risk for vitamin D deficiency: younger patients of both sexes, those who are not housebound, and nonimmigrants.[65] Many eating disorder patients also have been diagnosed with *fibromyalgia* and other nonspecific pain syndromes. Testing for vitamin D deficiency should be considered for these patients as well.

Cancers whose risk is inversely related to exposure to UVB sunlight and vitamin D levels: Colon cancer; breast, ovarian and prostate cancer; bladder, rectal, renal, uterine, cervical, gall bladder, laryngeal, oral, and pancreatic cancer, and Hodgkin's and non-Hodgkin's lymphoma

---

There are two molecules that are commonly referred to as "vitamin D": vitamin D_2 (ergocalciferol), derived by the effect of ultraviolet radiation on the ergosterol found in plants and other fungi, and vitamin D_3 (cholecalciferol), produced by a series of conversions that begins with the action of sunlight on the skin and ends with the conversion of 25-hydroxy-vitamin D to 1,25 (OH)2 D_3 in the kidney. 25-hydroxy vitamin D is what is measured in the blood; however, 1,25 (OH)2 D_3 is the active form of the vitamin that is involved in maintaining normal blood levels of calcium and phosphorus and in aiding in calcium absorption and bone mineralization.

Sources of Vitamin D: There are relatively few dietary sources of vitamin D. They include foods fortified with vitamin D, fish, eggs, and pastry products. Vitamin D can also be derived by exposure of skin to UVB rays in sunlight, which is affected by geographical location and can vary widely among individuals.

Deficiency of vitamin D in young people can affect their ability to reach peak bone mass.[66] Factors contributing to vitamin D deficiency include lack of sufficient sunlight, especially in northern countries during winter; poor nutrition; extreme diets; poverty; living in urban areas; and nonwhite ethnicity.

What we know about vitamin D:

- In the absence of vitamin D deficiency, vitamin D supplementation in young postmenopausal women does not significantly affect bone mineral density (BMD).
- Supplementation with vitamin D alone is not sufficient to prevent fractures in elderly populations; supplementation in this population must be at least 700-800 IU to reduce the risk of nonvertebral fractures.[67]
- Protein-energy malnutrition is a risk factor for bone loss, osteoporosis, and fracture.[68]
- A diet high in fruits and vegetables (which has a lower acid load) has been shown to be beneficial on the markers of bone metabolism and bone loss in children and adults.[69 70 71]

A recent study by Armas et al.[72] compared the efficacy of vitamins D_2 and D_3. The study found that while both produced similar increases in serum concentration of 25-hydroxy vitamin D after administration, vitamin D_3 produced a more sustained increase, peaking at fourteen days, while the effect of vitamin D_2 was less sustained. Vitamin D_2 potency was estimated at one-third that of vitamin D_3.

Serum 25OHD is the accepted blood test for measurement of status of vitamin D nutrition. Raising serum 25OHD has been shown to increase absorption of calcium, reduce fall frequency, and lower the risk of fractures in osteoporotic individuals. This study challenged the prevailing wisdom that vitamins D_2 and D_3 are equivalent, especially in light of increasing incidence of conditions due to vitamin D deficiency such as rickets, and indicates that reconsideration should be made regarding recommending vitamin D_2 over D_3.

Special risks in eating disorder patients for osteoporosis include the following:

1. Anorexic girls (ages thirteen to twenty-three) who also suffer from depression may be at higher risk for osteoporosis than those without depression. The reason is not known.[73]
2. Amenorrhea in anorexic women and young girls may indicate the onset of estrogen deficiency, which can have a negative effect on bone density and peak bone mass.
3. Undernutrition can affect bone density through deficiency of anabolic hormones such as insulinlike growth factor I (IGF-I). In addition, low weight is also a risk factor for lowered bone mass.[74] Other studies have shown that nutritional factors far outweigh the impact on bone mass of endocrinological factors such as IGF-I.[75]

Digestive Therapies

Eating disorder patients commonly suffer from complaints of constipation, diarrhea, bloating, and other digestive symptoms. These symptoms can pose a significant barrier during the refeeding process.

Probiotics are supplements that contain beneficial bacteria or yeast and are used to replace or enhance the body's naturally occurring gut flora. Probiotics are present in some foods, one example being *lactobacillus* in yogurt. Probiotics in the gastrointestinal tract are affected by the use of antibiotics, excess alcohol or drugs, stress, and some diseases. Probiotics are used to manage lactose intolerance by converting lactose in foods such as milk and other dairy products to lactic acid, which is better tolerated. These lactic acid bacteria (LAB) have demonstrated anticancer effects because of their ability to bind with cancer-causing substances formed in cooked meat and to reduce the activity of an enzyme called beta-glucoronidase that produces carcinogens in the gut, possibly pointing to a role in colon cancer prevention.[76] [77] [78] LABs have also been shown to have a cholesterol-lowering benefit, possibly by breaking down bile in the gut and thus reducing its reabsorption (entering the blood as cholesterol). Foods containing LABs have been shown to decrease the inflammatory response, improve absorption of minerals, and improve immune function.[79]

The most common sources of probiotics in food are dairy products and foods fortified with probiotics. Probiotics are also available in capsule or tablet form. Double-walled capsules may be more effective because of their ability to elude destruction in stomach acid. Lactic acid bacteria are found in certain fermented foods such as kefir, yogurt, sauerkraut, and kimchi. The two most common probiotics are various species of Bifidobacterium and Lactobacillus.

Studies on probiotics that are specifically pertinent to eating disorders include:

1. A probiotic mixture used to treat irritable bowel syndrome was found to reduce abdominal pain, distension, flatulence (gas), and borborygmi (stomach growling).[80]

2. Probiotics used by those suffering from chronic constipation reduced severity of constipation and stool consistency after two weeks.[81]

Probiotics replace LAB's and their use in treating eating disorder patients can significantly reduce constipation and improve digestion and absorption of nutrients.

Bitters such as Gentian (*Gentiana lutea)* can be used to stimulate appetite and digestion by stimulating the digestive juices and, as a result, promoting production of saliva, stomach juices, and bile. Bitters also speed up the emptying of the stomach. They are used whenever there is sign of sluggish digestion such as dyspepsia and flatulence. Gentian is sometimes used with other digestives such as ginger and cardamom.

Herbs and Nutraceuticals for Specific Diagnoses

Valerian is an herb that was used in ancient Greece and China and is found in ancient records of Galen and Dioscorides and in early Chinese textbooks on herbs. *Valeriana officinalis* is the species used most frequently for medical purposes. It has been used in the United States to treat anxiety and insomnia since the 1940s. Valerian is made up of a number of different compounds and has a characteristic "stinky" odor. Research studies done on valerian to treat specific medical conditions include:

Anxiety and Depression
Several studies have demonstrated the effectiveness of valerian in reducing symptoms of anxiety under social stress in healthy volunteers.[82] In a double-blind placebo controlled trial and in comparison with Valium (2.5 mg three times daily), a valerian preparation standardized to 80 percent dihydrovaltrate significantly reduced Hamilton Anxiety Scale scores after four weeks in patients with generalized anxiety disorder;[83] valerian and kava kava were compared with each other and to placebo and were found to reduce objective measures of anxiety, including decreasing systolic blood pressure responsiveness and stress-induced increase in heart rate.[84] Evidence to support this use is rated as unclear.

A combination of valerian and Rose of Sharon (Hibiscus syriacus) was successfully used in treating depressed patients over a six-week period. In a separate six week double-blind study of a valerian/St. John's wort (SJW) combination done in 93 participants, a statistically significant improvement in depression was seen on all psychometric scales.[85]

Muscle Spasm

Valerian has been used in traditional medicine to treat "nervous stomach," colic, and stomach spasms. This use has been confirmed in animal models.

Insomnia

Multiple studies have supported the effectiveness of valerian for the treatment of insomnia. The most impressive of these was a multicenter study of more than eleven thousand patients with sleep-related problems that found self-reported improvements in 94 percent of those treated with valerian.[86] Other studies have shown valerian to be effective in elderly patients and poor sleepers. In more recent, well-designed studies, valerian was found to improve sleep latency and quality and to be effective in poor sleepers of both sexes and in young and old.[87] Valerian was rated better than placebo on the Clinical Global Impression Scale (a clinician-rated scale designed to assess global severity of illness and change in the clinical condition over time).[88] Valerian (600 mg) was found to be similar in its effects on sleep quality as prescription oxazepam (common name: Serax) (10 mg/day) with fewer side effects.[89] Valerian extract (at a dose of 100 mg three times daily) was also shown to improve sleep after benzodiazepine withdrawal. Common dosages in these studies ranged from 400 mg-900 mg of valerian extract per night. Peak effectiveness was reached either immediately or within fourteen days.[90]

Valerian in combination with hops was comparable to over-the-counter diphenhydramine (Benadryl) in improving self-reports of sleep quality in a randomized placebo-controlled clinical trial. Benadryl produced greater increases in sleep efficiency and total sleep time compared with placebo. The valerian-hops combination produced sleep improvements that were associated with improved quality of life in the treatment of mild insomnia.[91]

Benzodiazepine Withdrawal

Valerian is in the herbal category of relaxing and tonic nervines. Nervine tonics are important to enhance individuals' ability to cope with their lives and transform unhealthy problems. Nervine tonics are short-term tranquilizers. Other herbs with both properties include passionflower (*Passiflora incarnata)*, oatmeal *(Avena sativa)* and skullcap *(Scutellaria lateriflora)*. These herbs may be helpful in treating benzodiazepine withdrawal.[92]

Recommendations for using Valerian: Choose a major brand name and start with a minimum dosage of 600-900 mg taken thirty to sixty minutes before bedtime. Valerian can be combined with hops, lemon balm, and/or passionflower in some preparations that may enhance effectiveness. There have been some reports of toxicity to the liver in some of the combination products, though this is not believed to be due to valerian.

Side effects: valerian is generally well tolerated in recommended doses for up to six months. Potential side effects reported in fewer than 10 percent of patients in research studies include headache, stomach upset, dizziness, and low body temperature. Use for long periods of time may negatively affect sleep. There have been some reports of morning "hangover" when using high doses of valerian.

Drug-herb interactions: Theoretically, valerian may increase drowsiness of prescription drugs or herbs that cause sedation and valerian should not be taken when driving or operating heavy machinery. Withdrawal symptoms can occur with abrupt cessation when taking multi-gram doses of valerian.

CASE EXAMPLE:

Tara is a twenty-five-year-old white female from New Jersey who was admitted to an inpatient hospital for treatment of anorexia nervosa. The patient had had her own business as a personal trainer, but her office—and many of her clients—perished in 9/11. Tara had been a competitive gymnast since age five, and only a back injury kept her from competing in the Olympic trials at fifteen. During her gymnastic career, she was weighed before every practice by her coach and was expected to keep her weight under tight control. The patient reported shaming statements made by coaches if she gained weight and embarrassment associated with being weighed in front of other gymnasts. At age ten, Tara's parents divorced and Tara lived with her mother whom she described as "very controlling and judgmental." Tara had minimal contact with her father, who moved to another state and remarried. She reported verbal and emotional abuse by her coach, including constant comments about her weight and appearance and calling her "fatty." By age eleven, the patient had begun food restricting and when she wasn't working out in the gym, she began jogging and did 200 sit-ups several times daily. She reported that in her teenage years, another gymnast told her that she could eat whatever she wanted to if she knew how to "take care of it." She began purging, alternating with binge eating and restricting, at fifteen. She also used laxatives to decrease her weight the day before she was to be weighed. After her back injury and her missed Olympic bid, she was no longer considered a competitive gymnast. The patient was a cheerleader in high school and on the track team and ran up to fifteen miles a week to control her weight. She continued her ED behaviors during college, majoring in physical education. She was date raped in college and did not tell anyone because she had been drinking at the time and felt it was "my fault."

After college, she moved to New York City and started her business. Her back injury symptoms became more severe, and the patient went from specialist to specialist for treatment of her chronic pain. She was diagnosed with osteoarthritis in her knees and spine. By twenty-two, she was on daily doses of Hydrocodone for pain. She underwent two back surgeries without relief of pain and began to abuse her pain meds. After 9/11, patient's chronic pain increased as did her reliance on medications. She became less able to take care of herself and moved back home to live with her mother. At the time of her admission, Tara was taking up to forty-two Hydrocodone tablets daily, which she was able to purchase on the Internet. She suffered from chronic constipation from the narcotics. She continued to binge, purge, and restrict. She was unable to exercise to the degree she had in the past and resorted more and more to the use of laxatives (up to ten per day, three to seven days/week) and diet pills, which she also bought online. The patient complained of severe hair loss, fatigue, amenorrhea, a generalized rash to her trunk and extremities, depression, and anxiety. Her one-week dietary recall showed that she would fast for up to two days at a time and then binge and purge three to four times daily. She was taking the antidepressant Prozac and had been prescribed benzodiazepine (Klonopin) for her anxiety.

Tara was diagnosed with anorexia-binge/purge type. She was admitted at 82 percent of her Ideal Body Weight (IBW). The patient presented with severe depression and a Beck Depression Inventory score of 46. She expressed suicidal ideation without a plan or true intent. Her laboratory testing showed electrolyte abnormalities and her EKG showed a slow heart rate. Tara was put on the opiate detox protocol using Subutex. After her detox period was completed, the patient was slowly tapered off benzodiazepines, using valerian to decrease withdrawal symptoms. Her supplement regimen included the following, with suggested brands listed:

1. For mood support:
   a. Prozac, which had worked well for her in the past
   b. omega-3 fatty acids, including EPA and DHA, to cover both her mood and cognitive issues at a beginning dose of 3 grams per day (approximately 1.5 grams of EPA and 1.5 grams of DHA) (Pro-Omega by Nordic Naturals)
   c. vitamin B complex, including B_{12} and folic acid (B-100 by Nature's Way)

2. For digestive support/constipation relief:
   a. digestive enzyme (Plantizyme by Thorne)
   b. Lactobacillus GG for constipation (Culturelle brand)
   c. Nutrient-dense diet with caloric intake increasing as tolerated

Follow Tara's case over the next few chapters to learn of her progress through treatment.

CHAPTER 4
PSYCHOLOGICAL TESTING OFFERS KEYS TO ED TREATMENT[93]

WITH JEANNETTE ROJAS[*]

"It is not...that some people do not know what to do with truth when it is offered to them, but the tragic fate is to reach, after patient search, a condition of mind-blindness, in which the truth is not recognized, though it stares you in the face."
Sir William Osler, physician (1849-1919)

Psychological testing—the key to your hand of cards. This chapter discusses the use of testing to help patients gain insight into their genetic makeup, personality strengths, and weaknesses and delves into the details of one case.

The Eating Disorder Inventory (EDI) was originally developed more than twenty years ago to test the "continuum model" of anorexia nervosa proposed by Nylander.[94]

---

[*] Ms. Jeannette Rojas is a clinical psychologist who specializes in eating disorders and is the primary therapist for the eating disorders program at Sierra Tucson Treatment Center. She served as the vice president of Avalon, Mexico City and Latin America's first center for eating disorders, a specialized treatment center exclusively dedicated to women suffering from eating disorders, trauma and addictions.

The EDI-3 is the first major revision of the test in almost fifteen years. It is the most widely used self-report measure of psychological traits or constructs shown to be clinically relevant in individuals with eating disorders. It is a standardized and easily administered measure yielding objective scores and profiles that are useful in case conceptualization and treatment planning for individuals with a confirmed or suspected eating disorder. The EDI-3 is not intended to yield a diagnosis; rather, it is aimed at the measurement of psychological traits or symptom clusters relevant to the development and maintenance of eating disorders.

The primary use of the EDI-3 is the clinical evaluation of symptomatology associated with eating disorders. It has the advantage of being standardized and economical, and does not require a trained interviewer.

The EDI-3 consists of ninety-one items organized in twelve primary scales and six composites. Three of the primary scales—Drive for Thinness (DT), Bulimia (B), and Body Dissatisfaction (BD)—are labeled Eating Disorder Risk Scales.

The remaining nine scales—Low Self-Esteem (LSE), Personal Alienation (PA), Interpersonal Insecurity (II),Interpersonal Alienation (IA), Interoceptive Deficits (ID), Emotional Dysregulation (ED), Perfectionism (P), Asceticism (A), and Maturity Fears (MF)—assess psychological constructs that have conceptual relevance to the development and maintenance of eating disorders.[95] Using the EDI-3 pre- and post-treatment could provide the therapist with important information for the course of treatment as well predictors of outcome.

This case illustrates how the EDI-3 could be used in developing a treatment plan as well as aftercare recommendations.

CASE EXAMPLE:

Paula is twenty-five and married. She came to inpatient treatment due to her eating disorder. She also reported being depressed and anxious.

At the age of fourteen, she went to a camp and started dieting and exercising compulsively, running up to two hours per day. When her family came to visit, they were alarmed at the marked reduction in her weight.

She started to see a nutritionist, but her symptoms increased. She was hospitalized and released. In college, she took nutrition classes and became an expert in counting calories and maintaining her calorie count below 1,200 a day. She started bingeing and purging two or more times a day and continued restricting.

Paula also had a history of drug abuse. She reported use of marijuana a year earlier as well as mushrooms, ecstasy, and LSD while she was in college and the use of alcohol two or three times per month. She also was diagnosed with depression. Even though she was on anxiety medication she reported extreme anxiety on a daily basis.

Paula also stated she was raped at age seventeen, an issue that she hadn't addressed before in treatment.

At the beginning of treatment, she said she didn't know if she could stand gaining weight and accept herself with a different body. She was her eating disorder and had difficulty seeing herself separate from her disease.

She had the following diagnosis:

Axis I: Anorexia nervosa (binge/purge type) with history of compulsive overexercising; polysubstance abuse (marijuana, ecstasy, mushrooms, and LSD) in remission; depression not otherwise specified (NOS) versus malnutrition-induced mood disorder; adjustment disorder with anxiety; history of rape at age seventeen; grief and loss issues; and history of emotional abuse.

Axis II: borderline features; dependent personality disorder.

Axis III: History of human papilloma virus (HPV) with normal Pap smear at present time; history of diarrhea alternating with constipation; possible irritable bowel syndrome; history of neck and back muscle spasm secondary to stress; history of dermatitis; and changes in vision thought secondary to Effexor; loss of enamel on teeth secondary to purging.

Axis IV: moderate marital stressors including dependency issues as well as dependency issues with family of origin.

Axis V: GAF (Global Assessment of Functioning) score of 55-60, indicative of moderate symptoms or moderate difficulty in one of the following: social, occupational, or school functioning.

Interpretation of Initial Test

Body Dissatisfaction: Paula had a T score of 39, which is low cinical range. This could reflect Paula's denial of her current clinical state. This scale is correlated to body weight and she was at 85 percent of IBW (ideal body weight).

Maturity Fears: The high score of 63 is consistent with Paula's fear of being an adult and accepting responsibility competes with her desire to stay a child and be taken care of.

According to a model proposed by Crisp, anorexia nervosa can serve as an adaptative function by reducing fear and anxiety associated with the biological and psychological challenges of development.[96]

Interpersonal Alienation: The Elevated Clinical range T score of 59 reflects Paula's lack of trust and closeness in relationships. When this range is elevated, it is likely due to sexual abuse, physical abuse, and a pattern of poor relationships with partners. This also reflects Paula's difficulties in making real connections with other people. This is important information because her lack of trust could be a challenge during the therapeutic process.

Perfectionism: The high T score of 62 in this scale suggests that Paula is experiencing some pressure from family or others to excel. Perfectionism is a trait that mantains her eating disorder, and her family didn't realize they were encouraging it.

Affective Problems Composite: The range on the T-score

of 55 and the elevation on the emotional dysregulation scale reflect marked mood shifts, mood instability, impulsivity, and general lability; this is common in patients who have had traumatic experiences.

At the beginning of treatment this was evident. Paula had difficulty accepting confrontations from peers in her group, which caused mood changes and her frequent desire to leave the group.

Overcontrol Composite: The elevated score of 55 on the Overcontrol Composite and elevated score of 60 on the Personal Alienation scale indicated a conflict between Paula's belief that she needed to maintain control all the time and her feelings of inadequacy associated with loss of control around her bingeing and purging at times.

Personal Alienation: this scale score also reflects feelings of feeling separate from others and losing out or of not being given due credit by others. Paula thought the group didn't like her and she had a difficult time at the beginning integrating with her peers.

Emotional Dysregulation: Paula had an elevated score of 55, which reflects tendencies toward poor impulse regulation, mood intolerance, and self-harm behaviors, which have been identified as poor prognostic signs. This could represent an obstacle during treatment because psychotherapy might bring intense emotions to the surface and Paula has a history of being unable to control her impulsivity in the past.

Interpretation of Testing at Discharge
Body Dissatisfaction: The increase in this score from low clinical to typical clinical reflects significant Body Dissatisfaction and discontent with body and shape as well as negative feelings regarding specific body regions.

This scale has three items that focus on the patient's perception of and feelings about her stomach that may be particularly sensitive for individuals who have fears associated with psychosexual development. At this point in treatment,

Paula was working on her rape.

During treatment, Paula was able to start talking about her rape and disclosed this issue to family members during family week. Paula minimized the significance of this event at the beginning of treatment but it became evident that the incident caused her to have memories, flashbacks, and nightmares. EMDR (Eye movement desensitization and reprocessing) sessions were important in working on this trauma issue.

The increase on the Body Dissatisfaction scale also reflects the difficulties associated with weight gain at discharge. She had an IBW of 80 percent at admission and of 90 percent at discharge. Paula continued to need significant support due to her fear of gaining weight. Another situation that might affect this difference in ranges was that Paula had a body imagery session a day prior to completing the last testing, in which issues relating to her discomfort with her body were discussed.

Maturity Fears: Upon discharge, the patient had a score of 39, which indicates acceptance of psychosexual maturity and adulthood. One of the goals in treatment was to overcome the fear of growing up and maturing. Frequently, patients agree to have this as a goal—wanting to be independent and make choices by themselves—even though their behavior will reflect the opposite. Paula grew in confidence in her ability to trust staff as well as her independence from her family during her treatment.

Affective Problems Composite: The T score of 31 is at a low clinical range suggesting no problems identifying, understanding or responding to an emotional state. Paula was able to sit in group while being confronted and not react. Also, she was able to use DBT (Dialectical Behavior Therapy) skills in order to cope with her emotions

Overcontrol Composite: The T score of 37 on a low clinical range indicates that she didn't demand the highest standard for performance. At this point of treatment she was not bingeing or purging, and was able to let go of control of aspects of her treatment.

Emotional Dysregulation: The move from a T score of 55

to T score for 39 in a low clinical range is an indicator of having less difficulty with mood instability, impulsivity, anger, and destructiveness.

This scale usually shows higher scores in eating disorder patients because the eating disorder symptoms play an important role in modulating the mood. Part of Paula's therapy was to focus on strategies to be able to tolerate and regulate negative emotions and mood.

Paula attended Dialectical Behavior Therapy (DBT) skills classes two hours every week during treatment. She struggled on and off with emotional dysregulation issues through treatment, especially after family week, and had a regression of behavior to a more dependent demeanor. However, she was able to apply DBT skills during this period to cope with these emotions.

In summary, the patient showed significant improvement across the board with her EDI-3 discharge test compared with the EDI-3 on admission. Having the EDI-3 pre- and postevaluation was an excellent tool to measure her progress and the areas that she needed to keep working on.

The clinical team recommended aftercare due to her perfectionism, body image issues, and ongoing difficulty in regulating emotions.

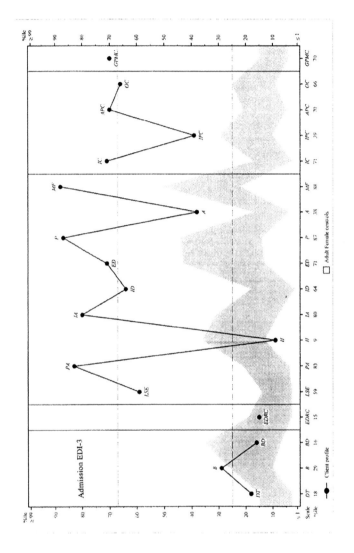

Note. Adult Combined Clinical Group: Low Clinical range = 1st - 24th %ile; Typical Clinical range = 25th - 66th %ile; Elevated Clinical range = 67th - 99th %ile.

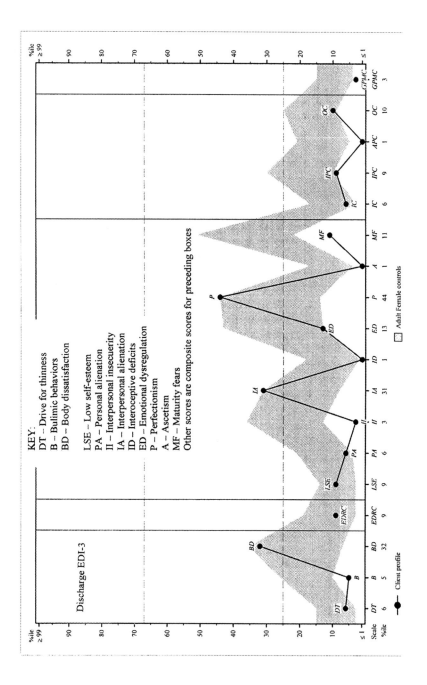

KEY:
DT – Drive for thinness
B – Bulimic behaviors
BD – Body dissatisfaction

LSE – Low self-esteem
PA – Personal alienation
II – Interpersonal insecuerity
IA – Interpersonal alienation
ID – Interoceptive deficits
ED – Emotional dysregulation
P – Perfectionism
A – Ascetism
MF – Maturity fears
Other scores are composite scores for preceding boxes

Discharge EDI-3

Adult Female controls

Client profile

CHAPTER 5
DIALECTICAL BEHAVIOR
THERAPY FOR ED PATIENTS

"The true test of character is not how much we know how to do, but how we behave when we don't know what to do."
John W. Holt Jr.

New skills for the new me: modifying dialectical behavior therapy (DBT) for eating disorder patients. This approach is examined as part of an integrative approach and its specific application to eating disorders.

D ialectical behavior therapy (DBT) was designed by Marsha Linehan[97] to treat those with borderline personality disorder or self-destructive behaviors. However, it is now used in eating disorder patients as well. DBT is a combination of cognitive behavioral therapy and Buddhist concepts of mindfulness. The therapy's purpose is to enable patients to learn to tolerate their pain, manage their emotions, and make a "life worth living." Included in DBT are the concepts of changing behaviors; validation of the client's reality, even when the therapist cannot agree with behaviors; acceptance of what cannot be changed; and "dialectics." Dialectics can be a complex idea to grasp but involves being able to hold two truths that may be conflicting at the same time. The purpose is to help clients get unstuck from rigid patterns of thinking or seeing the world.

DBT and Eating Disorders

A case report about a patient with bulimia showed that DBT training reduced binge eating and purging behaviors.[98] In a follow-up study by the same researchers, DBT treatment over twenty weeks was compared with patients being put on a wait list (control group) and the treatment group showed highly significant decreases in binge/purge behavior.

DBT in Practice

While few studies directly examine the effectiveness of DBT in ED, in practice DBT is anecdotally very effective in addressing the emotional dysregulation (emotional soup) for which an eating disorder is the maladaptive coping mechanism. Most ED patients have used restricting, bingeing, purging, exercise, drugs, alcohol, sex, or shopping to deal with their emotions. When they enter treatment and do not have access to these behaviors, they struggle to tolerate the onslaught of emotions and negative thoughts.

CASE EXAMPLE:

Marissa was thirty-one when admitted for treatment of anorexia, had used restricting and drugs to deal with the pain of a divorce, an enmeshed relationship with her father, and a chaotic relationship with her alcoholic mother. After going through detox for Ritalin, which she had been abusing for several years, she began to have feelings of insecurity, thinking that the other women in her group didn't like her or were talking about her behind her back. She alternated between isolating herself and acting out in her group (creating alliances that "split" the group). When she isolated, she missed sessions with her therapist or came to group late. This created chaos within the group structure and distracted her from focusing on her emotions. She had difficulty not constantly calling her ex-husband, and when she did give in to calling him she always felt less confident and angrier. When these feelings came up, she would begin to crave Ritalin, finding reasons why she should be put back on this prescription drug that she now denied abusing. Essentially, she had no resources beyond her ED and her addictions to help her cope with her emotional soup.

The first step in her use of DBT was focusing on the removal of life-threatening behaviors (her ED and drug abuse). The second step involved eliminating behaviors that interfered with treatment. In Marissa's case, this meant confronting her behaviors toward peers as well as her noncompliance with attending sessions and being late. Peers confronted her about her behaviors toward them and by their feedback validated her fear and anxiety. An example of such a conversation is:

"Marissa, when you do not show up for group on time, I feel fear and sadness."

"Marissa, I see your fear and anger and I can relate because when I first came into treatment I felt the same way."

These types of conversations led over time to an improvement in her relationship with peers. As this progressed, the patient learned to be more mindful of her emotions and to observe them without judgment or opinion, i.e., to unhook her emotions from the facts. For example:

Marissa: "When Mary and Joan were whispering at dinner, I felt left out and afraid that they were talking about me."

Therapist: "How did it feel for you when you noticed them talking?"

Marissa: "I felt fear and anger."

Therapist: "What interpretation did you make?"

Marissa: "That they didn't like me. That I wasn't good enough to be their friend."

Therapist: "Let's look at the facts. First, you saw Joan and Mary talking at dinner. Separate from this, you had an opinion that they were talking about you. Finally, you made a judgment that they felt you were not good enough to be their friend. These are three separate occurrences. They are not necessarily connected. How would you feel if you unhooked your opinion and judgment from the fact of seeing them talking?"

Marissa: "I might not feel so bad. I might wonder what they were talking about and go and ask them if I could join them."

DBT and Emotional Expression

A key principle of DBT is enabling patients to express their emotions and be in control of their emotions rather than their emotions controlling them and dictating their behaviors. The goal is not for patients to suffer in silence or become stoic and shut down, but to be in touch with their emotions in a sentient way. To do this, we can use the behavior chain analysis which enables patients to learn about what triggers their emotions; what their interpretations, body sensations, and emotions are; and what behaviors, emotions, and other consequences result.

More about Marissa

Marissa had a phone conversation with her ex-husband about visiting her son after discharge. During this conversation, he expressed concern about the possibility that Marissa might relapse and how this would affect their son. Marissa became enraged (and fearful), began screaming, and eventually hung up on him. The behavior chain analysis might look like this:

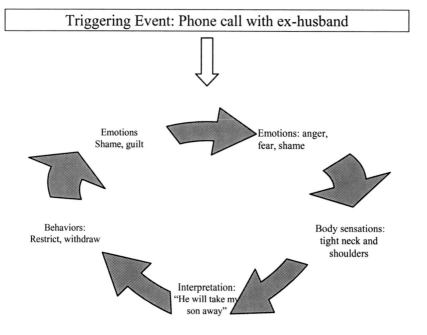

Triggering Event: Phone call with ex-husband

Emotions
Shame, guilt

Emotions: anger, fear, shame

Behaviors:
Restrict, withdraw

Body sensations:
tight neck and
shoulders

Interpretation:
"He will take my
son away"

This chain of events represents a vicious circle: reactions to events in ED patients' lives drive them to self-defeating behaviors, which continue to feed their emotional soup and then more self-defeating behaviors. It is important to teach patients that they can interrupt this circle and the earlier, the better. By recognizing bodily sensations related to their emotions, they can substitute healthier coping strategies for their current unhealthy ones.

DBT provides a number of effective coping strategies that are grouped into categories:

1. Mindfulness—teaches patients to be in the moment and observe, describe, and participate; teaches them to be nonjudgmental and one-mindful and to do what works.
2. Interpersonal effectiveness—teaches assertiveness and interpersonal problem –solving, including learning how to ask for what is needed, how to say no, and to cope with interpersonal conflict.

3. Distress tolerance—one of the most important modules, it enables patients to accept, find meaning for, and tolerate distress; to cope with crises; to accept what cannot be changed.
4. Emotion regulation—helps patients who experience intense emotions and who are sensitive to their own emotions and the emotions of those around them to identify and label their emotions, to recognize what might be in the way of changing their emotions, and to reduce sensitivity to emotions.

For example, Marissa could stay in the conversation with her ex-husband one-mindfully, without jumping to conclusions, and ask for what she needs.

"John, we have a custody agreement and I expect both of us to comply with this. My recovery is very important to me and so is our son. I don't want to do anything to jeopardize either."

To control emotions that will still come up after the phone call – fear of losing her son and anger at her ex-husband for trying to "control" her—Marissa could practice one of many skills that DBT teaches:

- breath work to help calm her nervous system
- pushing away and not focusing on events that have not happened yet
- taking a hot bath or sitting outside in nature; putting lavender lotion on her skin; meditating
- finding meaning: even though she is away from her son and misses him, she can reassure herself that being in treatment is for her and his best interest
- Imaging happy times in the past with her son and affirming that there are more times like this in the future.

Linehan's *Skills Training Manual for Treating Borderline Personality Disorder* is an excellent way to begin learning about DBT skills and how to teach them to clients. A non-

DBT-specific skill that helps patients to be less self-debasing is the exercise "ED me versus Non-ED me." In this assignment, patients are asked to draw a line down the middle of their notebook and on one side list all of the emotions, personality characteristics, behaviors, thoughts, etc. associated with their "ED self." On the other side, they are asked to list the same things associated with their "true self." The concept behind this is to allow patients to "dump" into the ED self all of the behaviors of which they feel most ashamed and guilty and to create a separate persona for this false self, even giving it a name. They can also be asked to draw both selves, again to enable them to begin to see themselves as separate from their disease. Here is Marissa's:[99]

ED me: "Janice the Witch"	Non-ED me: Marissa
I hate myself I am fat and disgusting I like to be in control I enjoy when people call me "sick"because that means I am thin I am jealous of other people Emotions: guilt, shame, fear, anger I don't have any friends My thighs and butt are too big I hate my breasts No one will love me unless I'm thin I should die so I won't cause anyone more pain I am not a good daughter or mother	I do have some good friends There are many people who care about me I like my eyes and my smile I am a good mother

Early in treatment, patients' list of "ED–me" characteristics will far outstrip their list of non-ED characteristics. When asked, Marissa reported that she felt she spent over 90 percent of her time and thoughts in the "ED me."

As time goes on, this percentage will reduce in direct relationship to the patient's progress in treatment and it is a good measure of how well a patient is doing in treatment.

DBT also includes an exercise called "Pros and Cons (of tolerating distress)" that enables patients to list the benefits and downsides to holding on to their disease. This assignment can be applied to their ED along with drug addiction, co-dependence, sex addiction, etc.

One of the most impactful distress tolerance skills is "radical acceptance," defined as acceptance from deep within. There is often something in a patient's life that stands in the way of her or him being completely free of the disease.

More on Marissa

In Marissa's case, her father's abandonment after her parents' divorce was a huge stumbling block. She was the youngest of five children and after her parents split, she rarely spent time with her father, but had always worshiped him as a child. Eventually, she became very angry at him and criticized him for leaving her and not taking an active role in her childhood despite living in the same city. When asked to think of one thing in her life that she found "impossible to accept," she had no trouble naming this situation. In working through the process of radical acceptance, Marissa was asked to do guided imagery. She was able to get in touch with a memory from age five when she and her father used to go skiing together and then afterwards they would stop at a local tea house on their way home and split a cookie and have hot chocolate. This memory was very clear for her and she was able to get in touch with the love and adoration she'd felt for her father at that age. Next, she was asked "what does the five-year-old Marissa want from Dad?"

Her response: "to be close to him, for him to love me." Once this imagery was complete, the patient was able to see that her adult feelings of anger stood in the way of something that was critically important to her inner child: the longing to have a relationship with her father. In future sessions, her anger at her father was validated and she was able to release the anger with EMDR,* anger work, and Somatic® Experiencing while staying in touch with the inner child's desire and love for her father. In working on radical acceptance, she realized that the child's desire for a relationship was strong and dominant over the adult's resentment and anger. In family week, Marissa was able to reconnect with her father and to satisfy her inner child while expressing in her communications with him her disappointment and hurt at feeling abandoned. The concept of radical acceptance—acceptance of something that at the time seemed unacceptable—enabled her to knock down a long-standing barrier to having a relationship with her father that had kept her stuck in feelings that fueled her self-defeating behaviors.

Overall, DBT training enables ED patients to learn and substitute healthy coping skills for their unhealthy behaviors. DBT training is a powerful tool in the treatment of ED patients because of its ability to enable and support patients in becoming empowered to have a life worth living.

---

* **Eye Movement Desensitization and Reprocessing (EMDR)** is a therapy used to treat the symptoms of post-traumatic stress disorder (PTSD) and other mental health problems using eye movements similar to those that occur during REM sleep

® **Somatic Experiencing** is a type of therapy used to treat PTSD, other physical trauma-related health problems and mental illness by using the body's perceived sensations. It was developed by Peter A. Levine and is described in his book *Waking the Tiger.*

CHAPTER 6
CORNERSTONES – TREATMENT OF DEPRESSION AND ANXIETY

"If you let go a little, you will have a little happiness. If you let go a lot, you will have a lot of happiness. If you let go completely, you will be free."
Jack Kornfield[100]

Depression and anxiety are significant diagnoses found in ED patients. While many depressed patients can experience disordered eating, a larger percentage of ED patients suffer from mood disorders. Just as the use of alcohol and other drugs of abuse can cause mood disorders, undernutrition can contribute to their occurrence. Use of herbal therapies may reduce side effects of prescription medications. These therapies often are better tolerated and can enhance the effectiveness of traditional antidepressant therapy.

T reatment of Major Depressive Disorder (MDD) has changed dramatically over the past fifty years with the advent of new categories of medication and the development of the biological model of depression that views MDD as a condition caused by deficiencies in brain chemicals known to be related to mood: dopamine, norepinephrine and serotonin. However, research on the efficacy of medications for the treatment of depression has been less than unanimous in showing efficacy. For example, a controversial study published in 1998 reviewed studies on 2,318 patients who had been randomly assigned to either antidepressant medication or placebo in nineteen double-blind clinical trials. This study concluded that the data "raise the possibility that the apparent drug effect (25% of the drug response) is actually an active placebo effect. Examination of pre-post effect sizes among depressed individuals assigned to no-treatment or wait-list control groups suggest that approximately one-quarter of the drug response is due to the administration of an active medication, one-half is a placebo effect, and the remaining quarter is due to other nonspecific factors."[101] While the method of analysis in this review was questioned by the psychiatric community, it was not the first to question the efficacy of prescription antidepressant medications. Walsh et al. emphasized the importance of including placebo groups in clinical trials of new antidepressant medications because of the potential placebo effect in treating MDD. In their review of controlled trials between 1981 and 2000, patients responded to placebo 10 to 50 percent of the time; in half of the studies, 30 percent or more of patients had clinically significant improvements in their depression by taking a placebo pill. This placebo response may just show the course of depression with the passage of time.[102] Therefore, despite numerous studies on the effectiveness of antidepressant medication, there is still more that needs to be understood.

Herbs and other nutraceuticals have been used for some time in the treatment of depression and anxiety. There has been substantial research in more recent times that supports the efficacy of these natural treatments of depression and the potential that they may support and enhance the efficacy of prescription medications. A factor of note is that their use is associated with very few serious side effects compared with the use of prescription antidepressant therapy.

Another factor in depression that is not usually taken

into account in conventional approaches to the treatment of MDD or other mood disorders is that malabsorption of nutrients is an important cause of depression and even marginal deficits of certain nutrients have been linked to depression. This fact is particularly important in ED patients who are chronically undernourished or malnourished. Essential fatty acids (omega-3 fatty acids) and vitamin B_{12} and folic acid have a multifactorial effect on mood as noted in the previous chapter. Depletion of the amino acids tryptophan (the precursor of serotonin), phenylalanine and tyrosine (precursors of norepinephrine and dopamine) have been shown to depress mood.[103] Impaired digestion in ED patients can contribute to these deficiencies and, traditionally, patients with depression have slowed digestion, further complicating this issue. This sets the stage for a more vital role for the use of complementary and alternative therapies in the treatment of depression.

One of the challenges in using herbs/botanicals is that these plants contain numerous ingredients and the "active" compound(s) may not be known. To make a preparation that is "standardized" or contains not only exactly what it is supposed to contain but in the exact same amounts is a difficult proposition for manufacturers. The location and environment in which plant medicines are grown also influences the ability of manufacturers to standardize their preparations. For example, St. John's wort must be harvested between July and August and dried immediately to avoid loss of potency.[104] When choosing an herbal preparation, it is important to pay attention to whether the product has been "standardized" to the best-known active ingredient. Also important is the choice of manufacturer. It's generally safer to choose well-known, established companies or to choose the preparation that has been shown to be effective in research studies. Below are several nutraceuticals that have been shown to be as effective as prescription antidepressants. The discussion of these therapies is not meant to be exhaustive. References are included for more detailed information.

St. John's Wort (Scientific name: Hypericum perforatum L.)

St. John's wort (SJW) is a plant native to Europe but also found in the United States and Canada. Ancient Greeks used it, as did Hippocrates, for its anti-inflammatory and healing uses. It derives its name from St. John the Baptist, around whose birthday, June 24, it is usually found to be in bloom. SJW has been used in traditional medicine as an antidepressant or diuretic and for the treatment of gastritis (inflammation of the stomach) and insomnia. Oil made from SJW ("red oil") was thought to be particularly effective as a topical treatment for hemorrhoids. The medicinal parts of SJW are the flower and, to a lesser degree, the leaves. There are numerous active chemicals in SJW, including melatonin. Until recently, hypericin was thought to be the most active constituent in SJW; however newer research suggests that another constituent, *hyperforin,* may play a major role in its antidepressant activity due to its modulating effects on serotonin, dopamine, and noradrenaline. It also has been shown to inhibit the uptake of GABA, another brain chemical implicated in depression. It is recommended that SJW preparations be standardized to 3 percent hyperforin to improve efficacy and potency. SJW has been used for treating depression, dysthymia, anxiety, mood disorders associated with menopause, obsessive-compulsive disorder (OCD), attention deficit hyperactivity disorder (ADHD), and seasonal affective disorder (SAD). SJW is available without a prescription and is a leading treatment for depression in Germany.

Research: SJW has strong scientific evidence for its use in the treatment of mild to moderate depression. The research evidence is still unclear for the use of SJW for anxiety, obsessive-compulsive disorder, menopausal mood disorders, premenstrual syndrome, and seasonal affective disorder.

Two high-quality research studies in the United States on SJW did not show it to be effective for treating depression. However, questions have been raised regarding the quality of the studies' design and so these studies cannot be considered completely valid.

Most of the studies on St. John's wort have been done in Germany. As noted in the previous chapter, valerian in combination with either St. John's wort or Rose of Sharon was effective in reducing symptoms of mild depression. A Medline review of randomized clinical trials, of which twenty were double-blind, showed St. John's wort in a dose of 300 to 1,000 mg/day over two to twelve weeks to be two times better than placebo and more effective than conventional prescription antidepressants. Fewer than 20 percent of those taking SJW had side effects, compared with an almost 53 percent rate of side effects for conventional antidepressant therapies.[105] The Cochrane database[106] reviewed thirty-seven studies on SJW, including twenty-six placebo-controlled studies and fourteen comparing SJW with standard antidepressants. SJW was shown to be slightly better than placebo in the treatment of mild to moderate depression when compared with selective serotonin reuptake inhibitors (SSRIs) and tricyclic antidepressants.[107 108 109 110 111] In trials restricted to those with major depression, the combined response ratio (RR) varied from 1.15 (slightly better than placebo) to 2.09 (two times better than placebo). In trials that were not restricted in this way, the RR varied from 1.71-6.13. SJW was as effective as standard antidepressant therapy. The SJW–treated participants had fewer side effects. Reviewers felt that variability in quality of preparations of SJW could have influenced the statistical significance of the results.[112] In a review of alternative treatments for unipolar depression in women, Manber et al. concluded that exercise, stress, reduction, bright light exposure, and sleep deprivation "hold greater promise as adjuncts to conventional treatment than as monotherapies for major depression. The evidence to date is not sufficiently compelling to suggest the use of SJW in favor of or as an alternative to existing U.S. FDA regulated compounds. Initial evidence suggests that acupuncture might be an effective alternative mono-therapy for major depression, single episode."[113]

Still, the effectiveness of SJW in treating moderate to severe depression was disputed until more recent studies such as a 2005 randomized, controlled double-blind study in which SJW (900 mg/day) was compared with paroxetine (brand name: Paxil) at 20 mg once a day. No placebo group was used due to ethical considerations of failing to treat patients with moderate or severe depression. The study results showed SJW to be at least as effective as Paxil in treating moderate to severe depression over six weeks. Effectiveness was defined as a 50 percent reduction in the HAM-D scores. Seventy percent of participants responded to SJW versus 60 percent for the paroxetine group; and 50 percent of patients in the SJW went into remission versus 35 percent for the paroxetine group. In patients who did not respond initially to a dose of 900 mg/day, increasing the dose to 1,800 mg/day after two weeks proved more beneficial compared to an increase in paroxetine to 40 mg/day. Significantly, side effects did not increase with the increased dose of SJW. This study was well designed, avoiding pitfalls of a previous study that was underpowered and strongly supported the use of SJW (extract WS 5570) in the treatment of moderate to severe depression.[114] SJW WS 5570 is sold under the brand name Perika by Nature's Way.

SJW was tested versus placebo to treat social phobia, and there was no evidence to support its use in this condition.[115] SJW was found to be more effective than and as safe as placebo in the treatment of somatization disorders.[116]

St. John's Wort Side Effects, Interactions, and Dosage

There are herb-drug interactions to consider in using SJW (see below). Despite these label side effects, studies to date have generally shown that there is a lower incidence of all adverse events with SJW when compared with standard antidepressants. Side effects include gastrointestinal upset, skin rashes, fatigue or sedation, anxiety and restlessness, sexual dysfunction (including impotence), headache, dizziness, and dry mouth. These symptoms occur in approximately 1 to 3 percent of patients who take SJW, similar to side effects with placebo and much less than with standard antidepressant therapy.[117]

Drug Herb Interactions with St. John's wort:

1. reduces the effect of the heart medicine Digitalis.
2. may increase effect and side effects of other drugs or herbs that increase serotonin (5-HTP, SAMe, SSRIs, Robitussin DM).
3. may increase the effect of Xanax, coumadin, and immunosuppressive agents.
4. may decrease effectiveness of the oral contraceptive pill.
5. may increase metabolism of the seizure medicine Dilantin.
6. may reduce levels of the lipid-lowering medicine Zocor but has no effect on Pravacol or Lescol. Its effect on Lipitor or Mevacor is unknown.
7. may induce mania in bipolar patients.

SAMe *(Scientific name: S-adenosyl-L-methionine)*

SAMe is a molecule produced in yeast cell cultures and found in all living cells. SAMe contributes to the synthesis, activation, and metabolism of hormones, neurotransmitters, nucleic acids, proteins, phospholipids, and certain drugs. SAMe is also a precursor to the amino acids cysteine, taurine, and glutathione. It was discovered in Italy in 1952 and has been available by prescription in Europe since 1975 for the treatment of arthritis and depression.

 Research:

Depression - In a study using brain wave testing electroencephalograms (EEGs) and event-related potentials (ERPs) and low-resolution brain electromagnetic tomography (LORETA), intravenous administration of SAMe when compared with placebo produced typical changes in the brain consistent with other antidepressants and in the regions of the brain critical to the efficacy of antidepressants.[118]

Increased blood concentrations of SAMe also were associated with enhanced mood in patients with depression. A meta-analysis of studies that compared SAMe with placebo or tricyclic antidepressants found SAMe to be more efficacious than placebo and comparable to tricyclics.[119]

A summary of forty-two studies on SAMe and depression, of which twenty-eight were of sufficient quality to be included in this review, showed that SAMe compared with placebo produced a decrease in the HAM-D of 6 points at three weeks. Compared with traditional antidepressant drugs, SAMe was not associated with a statistically significant difference in outcomes, i.e., was comparable to these therapies.[120]

Alpert and colleagues demonstrated that SAMe can also be useful in augmenting the effectiveness of other antidepressants in patients in whom treatment with SSRIs or venlafaxine was not sufficient to ameliorate depression. SAMe participants already taking a standard antidepressant had a 50 percent response rate and a remission rate of 43 percent on the HAM-D. This trial was not placebo-controlled and therefore further studies are warranted.[121]

Osteoarthritis

This use was found when patients with depression who were taking SAMe noted improvement in their symptoms of osteoarthritis. SAMe is a painkiller similar to nonsteroidal anti-inflammatories (NSAIDs) such as Ibuprofen and the COX-2 inhibitor Celebrex (celecoxib). The results of extensive clinical trials that enrolled about 22,000 patients with osteoarthritis showed SAMe to have effectiveness similar to that of nonsteroidal anti-inflammatory drugs, but SAMe was better tolerated with fewer side effects.[122] A two-year study in patients with osteoarthritis of the knee, hip, and spine using SAMe demonstrated improvement in the severity of patient symptoms (morning stiffness, pain at rest, and pain on movement) with minimal side effects. SAMe also improved the depressive symptoms associated with osteoarthritis.[123]

SAMe was compared with the COX-2 inhibitor celecoxib in a double-blind crossover trial for pain control in patients with osteoarthritis of the knee. In the first month of the study, celecoxib showed more pain reduction than SAMe; by the second month, there was no difference in pain between the SAMe and celecoxib groups.[124]

Treatment with SAMe may require up to thirty days to achieve maximum effect as opposed to fifteen days with NSAIDs. This indication can be particularly useful in treating eating disorder patients who have been compulsive exercisers and have evidence of osteoarthritis.

Fibromyalgia

SAMe was found in several clinical trials to be helpful in treating fibromyalgia with reductions in trigger points and pain as well as improvements in mood and morning stiffness.[125]

Liver Function

SAMe is the primary source of glutathione, a compound that is involved in the detoxification process in the liver. SAMe can be beneficial in improving liver function in cirrhosis and intrahepatic cholestasis associated with acute or chronic liver diseases. Multiple short-term clinical studies have demonstrated the effectiveness of short-term SAMe (compared with placebo) to decrease pruritus (itching), fatigue, and liver function tests in blood.[126] [127] SAMe should be considered in treating alcoholic patients with or without liver disease.

Migraine Headaches and ADHD
SAMe has also been shown to be beneficial in treating migraine headaches at a dose of 200-400 mg twice daily and to help in regulating sleep. Preliminary evidence suggests that SAMe may lessen symptoms of **attention deficit hyperactivity disorder** (ADHD), but more evidence is needed in support of this.

 SAMe Side Effects, Interactions, and Dosage

Side effects
When taken orally, SAMe can cause gastrointestinal upset, including gas, nausea, vomiting, diarrhea, and constipation. Other side effects can include mild insomnia, sweating, dizziness, nervousness, and headache. Hypomania can occur in bipolar patients, and one case of mania with suicidal ideation was reported in an otherwise healthy patient.[128]

Interactions
- SAMe can increase the effects and side effects of other products that increase serotonin (5-HTP, L-tryptophan, and SJW).
- Concurrent use with prescription drugs that increase serotonin such as SSRIs and tricyclics; Monoamine oxidase inhibitors; or the painkillers Talwin, Demerol, and Ultram can cause a serotoninlike syndrome with symptoms including agitation, tremors, anxiety, tachycardia, diarrhea, hyperreflexia, shivering, and cold sweats.

- Theoretically, concurrent use of SAMe and Robitussin DM can increase risk of serotonin syndrome.
- SAMe may reduce the effectiveness of Levodopa given to patients with Parkinson's Syndrome, leading to an increase in the symptoms of this disease
- SAMe can convert bipolar patients from a depressive to a manic state.

Dosage

The starting dose for depression is 400-1,600 mg per day. For osteoarthritis, use 200 mg three times daily. For alcoholic liver disease or cirrhosis, oral doses of 1,200-1,600 mg per day have been used. For fibromyalgia, 800 mg per day is the starting dose.[129]

SAMe comes in two forms: butanedisulfonate and tosylate. The butanedisulfonate form is five times more bioavailable than the more commonly sold tosylate form, and questions have been raised about the stability of the tosylate form. Pharmaton sells the butanedisulfonate form. [130]

5-Hydroxytryptophan (5-HTP)

5-HTP is related to the amino acid L-tryptophan and to serotonin. Because tryptophan has a controversial history and because it is the precursor amino acid to 5-HTP, its use, side effects, and actions will be discussed along with those of its metabolite, 5-HTP. In the body, L-tryptophan is converted to 5-HTP which can then be converted to serotonin. It readily crosses the blood-brain barrier and increases central nervous system (CNS) synthesis of serotonin. Tryptophan is an amino acid that is essential to human nutrition. It cannot be synthesized in the body and so must be obtained from the diet. Amino acids are the building blocks of protein. Tryptophan is the precursor for serotonin, melatonin, and niacin.

Tryptophan has been implicated as both a possible cause of

schizophrenia and an aid for schizophrenic patients. When the body does not metabolize it, it can lead to buildup of a waste product that is toxic to the brain. Food sources include chocolate, oats, bananas, dairy products, turkey, fish, meat, chicken, peanuts, and sesame seeds.

Tryptophan has been used in the past as a sleep aid. In 1989, a large outbreak of a debilitating and sometimes fatal autoimmune illness called eosinophilia myalgia syndrome (EMS) was traced to certain formulations of tryptophan. A Japanese manufacturer, Showa Denko KK, in an attempt to cut costs, eliminated one step in its purification process, thereby allowing a toxic contaminant into the end product. As a result, tryptophan was banned for sale in the United States. During this same time, Prozac was released on the market. In 2001, tryptophan sale restrictions were loosened and it is now sold mainly through compounding pharmacies or mail order retailers.[131] The U.S. Food and Drug Administration official paper on L-Tryptophan states: "(Animal studies) showed that some, but not all, of the pathologic effects associated with EMS were caused by contaminants." The FDA "raised questions regarding the safety of high doses of uncontaminated L-tryptophan." An import alert continues to limit the importation of L-tryptophan into the United States.[132]

 Research: 5-HTP has been extensively studied for a number of purposes, including the treatment of binge eating associated with obesity, depression, fibromyalgia, and chronic headaches and as a sleep aid. It is well absorbed orally with approximately 70 percent of the oral dose ending up in the bloodstream. It easily crosses the blood-brain barrier, increasing production of serotonin in the central nervous system (CNS).[133]

Depression

A Cochrane review of tryptophan and 5-HTP in the treatment of depression identified 108 trials, of which only two were of sufficient quality to be included. Those two studies had only sixty-four patients and the conclusion reached was: "The available evidence suggests these substances were better than placebo at alleviating depression." The researchers stated that more studies were needed to rule out the possible association between these studies and EMS.[134]

A 2004 article in Toxicology Letter noted that "no definitive cases of toxicity have emerged despite worldwide usage of 5-HTP for the last 20 years, with the possible exception of one unresolved case of a Canadian woman."[135]

Anxiety

One small study examined ten outpatients with anxiety states who were treated with L-5-HTP and carbidopa. There was a significant reduction in anxiety on three different anxiety scales.[136]

Obesity

Another use of 5-HTP is in the treatment of binge eating associated with obesity. Cangiano et al. (1992)[137] showed that supplementation with 900 mg of 5-HTP when compared with placebo in a double-blind study with and without diet prescription decreased appetite, produced weight loss in obese patients, reduced carbohydrate intake, and increased early satiety. These study results were confirmed in a separate study for a longer period of time (two consecutive six-week periods).[138] Similar results were achieved in noninsulin dependent diabetics.[139]

A question is often raised as to the sexual side effects of 5-HTP, given its function of increasing serotonin. There are no reports in the literature specifically addressing this issue. Anecdotally, there has been no report of sexual side effects in the doses commonly used.

5-HTP Side Effects, Interactions, and Dosage
5-HTP can be taken 50 mg three times daily for depression or 100-200 mg at bedtime for depression and insomnia. It can be taken with or without food. The dose in fibromyalgia is 100 mg three times daily. Dosages of 300 mg three times daily are used for treatment of obesity.

CAUTION: for persons taking conventional antidepressants that increase serotonin, use of 5-HTP in high doses may contribute to the development of serotonin syndrome. There has been one report of three patients who developed stroke after using serotonergic drugs (Call-Fleming) syndrome.[140] Because of the history of contamination of L-tryptophan products in the past, it would be wise to choose products of 5-HTP from reputable manufacturers.

L-Theanine

L-theanine (LT) is an amino acid found in green tea and has been primarily used as a relaxant.

Research:
Anxiety – A study by Lu et al. (2004) compared LT with the prescription antianxiety agent alprazolam (Xanax) and with placebo. (Xanax is a commonly used, short-acting benzodiazepine). The double-blind placebo-controlled study measured anxiety in healthy volunteers who were exposed to an experimentally induced anxiety-provoking (anticipatory anxiety) situation. Results on the Beck Anxiety Inventory, State-Trait Anxiety Inventory, and the Visual Analog Mood Scale (VAMS) showed that while L-theanine had some relaxing effects during the relaxation phase, neither LT nor Xanax demonstrated any antianxiety effects during the anticipatory anxiety phase.[141]

L-theanine's effect on psychological and physiological

stress was the subject of a double-blind, placebo-controlled study. Results showed that LT intake resulted in decreased heart rate and salivary immunoglobulin A (a marker for stress response in the body). This study suggested that LT produced attenuation of the sympathetic nervous system response to stress.[142]

CASE EXAMPLE: More on Tara

Tara tolerated benzodiazepine and opiate withdrawal well. However, she had been dependent on these two medications to help her sleep. She suffered from disruptive sleep, waking often throughout the night and not feeling refreshed in the mornings. She was compliant with meals. Tara was not allowed to exercise until she had reached 85 percent of her Ideal Body Weight. During refeeding, she continued to have small, hard stools. Bone density testing showed osteopenia in her spine with a normal bone density in the hips. Psychological testing showed Axis 1 diagnosis of major depressive disorder and polysubstance abuse; she had Axis II diagnoses of borderline personality disorder and self-defeating personality traits. Further testing showed that Tara met DSM-IV criteria for posttraumatic stress disorder.

Tara attended a grief group and presented a letter on sadness and anger associated with her gymnastics career. She also presented an anger letter to her rapist. She began to address issues relating to her abuse of diet pills and narcotics, completing her 1st Step for both. Tara also continued to experience craving for pain pills and exhibited drug-seeking behavior on several occasions during the first month of treatment. Tara had EMDR and Somatic Experiencing to begin to work on her trauma. She began to address the rape and her trauma from 9/11. She experienced release of trauma from her body and began learning the technique of resourcing (coping skills used to reduce the nervous system activation associated with trauma). Specific prescriptions for

CAM therapies included:

1. Good nutrition and a regimen of dietary supplements increased her appetite and decreased bloating. She was advised to continue the omega-3-FAs, which may help with borderline personality symptoms.
2. Tara was placed on calcium and magnesium for bone protection (Cal-Mag-Citrate by Thorne). Magnesium also helps with constipation.
3. Tara was prescribed a weight-bearing exercise program for osteopenia.
4. She was referred to acupuncture for pain management, drug cravings and for help with constipation.
5. Tara was prescribed SAMe for depression and osteoarthritis pain. She had no evidence of bipolar disorder. Because of a possible advantage in pain management of SAMe (brand Pharmaton), Tara was put on a dose of 200 mg twice daily after discontinuation of Prozac.
6. She was prescribed 5-HTP for depression and sleep at a dosage of 100 mg at bedtime. The patient reported "I'm dreaming again."

CHAPTER 7
COPING WITH STRESS:
AN INTEGRATIVE MEDICINE
PERSPECTIVE

*"Develop a mind that is vast like the water, where experiences both
pleasant and unpleasant can appear and disappear without
conflict, struggle, or harm. Rest in a mind like vast water."*
Buddha

Stress has been implicated in many disease processes. Recent
research has demonstrated the role of stress in the development
of eating disorders and mood disorders and in the maintenance
of substance use disorder.

U nder stress, the body goes through a very well-defined
series of reactions that at first enable us to deal with
stress through fighting, fleeing, or freezing. These reactions are
part of our primitive brain, the oldest part of the human
neuroanatomy. It's essentially unchanged from caveman days.
However, if the stressor is chronic, the very lifesaving stress
reaction becomes a detriment, causing wear and tear to the
body and affecting key survival systems such as the immune
system.
   There is a high rate of comorbidity in eating disorders with
mood disorders including depression and anxiety, substance
use disorders (SUD), and PTSD. What these disorders have in

common is the shared mechanism of the stress response.

In a sample of 2,436 female inpatients treated over a five-year period for anorexia, bulimia, and eating disorder not otherwise specified (ED-NOS), 97 percent had one or more comorbid diagnoses. Ninety-four percent had mood disorders, primarily unipolar depression; 56 percent had anxiety disorders; and 22 percent had substance use disorders. Alcohol use was twice as likely in bulimics as in anorexics or ED-NOS patients; polysubstance use was three times more prevalent in bulimics; OCD was two times more likely with anorexics; and PTSD was twice as prevalent with binge-purge anorexia. Psychoses including schizophrenia were three times more likely with restricting anorexics and twice as prevalent with binge-purge anorexics.[143] In another study, alcohol use disorders (AUDs) were associated with the presence of major depression, anxiety disorders, and cluster B personality disorder symptoms. AUDs were also associated with personality traits of impulsivity and perfectionism.[144]

The stress reaction is triggered when there is childhood trauma. The link between trauma and eating disorders has been demonstrated in a number of studies. In contrast to normal eaters, bulimic women reported higher levels of childhood abuse and higher psychopathology. In the bulimics, severity of current psychopathology corresponded to the presence and severity of childhood abuse.[145] In a study of BED patients, 83 percent reported some form of childhood maltreatment; 59 percent reported emotional abuse, 36 percent reported physical abuse, 30 percent reported sexual abuse, 69 percent reported emotional neglect, and 49 percent reported physical neglect. Of all forms of abuse, only physical neglect led to dietary restraint in women. Emotional abuse tended to result in more body dissatisfaction, higher depression, and lower self-esteem in men and women; sexual abuse was associated with greater body dissatisfaction in men.[146] In morbidly/extremely obese patients seeking bariatric surgery, 69 percent reported childhood maltreatment; 46 percent, emotional abuse; 29 percent, physical abuse; 32 percent, sexual abuse; and 49 percent, emotional abuse.[147] Research has also shown a definite relationship between childhood trauma and psychological problems and physical illness in later life. These illnesses include eating disorders, substance abuse, phobias, multiple personality disorders, irritable bowel syndrome, rheumatoid arthritis, and autoimmune disorders. Posttraumatic stress disorder (PTSD) is being recognized as a possible mediating variable in these connections.[148]

In the overweight ED patient, the chronic release of the stress hormone cortisol promotes the release of insulin, the hormone of fat storage. Stress, therefore, contributes directly to weight gain.

Patients with PTSD and patients with ED share the phenomenon of hyperactivity of the hypothalamic-pituitary - adrenal (HPA) Axis with its attendant cascade of neurohormonal changes. HPA Axis hyperactivity is thought to be permanent and shows up clinically as increased sensitivity to even minor stressors later in life.

Further, there is a link between trauma, eating disorders, and mood disorders. In a study of 400 female undergraduates, depression was found to be strongly associated with emotional abuse, and emotional abuse was significantly associated with bulimia. After controlling for the other variable tested in this study dissociation, emotional abuse, and depression together were significantly associated with bulimia; depression was felt to be the mediating factor for the association between emotional abuse and bulimia (i.e., emotional abuse → depression → bulimia).[149] The stress hormone cortisol has been shown to be elevated in depression (just as it is elevated in ED and PTSD).

The ED patient who uses drugs or alcohol to self-medicate is further activating the HPA Axis. It is thought that the dopaminergic system in the brain is the area activated at the initiation of addictions. Recently, the stress reaction has been implicated in the <u>maintenance</u> of the addictions and as a factor in relapses. In the overweight ED patient, the chronic release of the stress hormone cortisol affects the release of insulin, the hormone of fat storage. The link between obesity and stress is also becoming clearer. Any chronic illness such as an eating disorder or addictions can trigger the body's stress response.

Cortisol is also elevated in patients with depression.

What is stressful depends on personal perception. Previous experience can prepare us to cope better or serve as a trigger for the stress response if the prior experience was similar in nature and traumatic. Information can help us be more aware of impending stressful events.

Differences in reacting to stress also result from personality differences that affect coping styles; avoidant people differ radically in their responses compared with those who emotionally detach in times of stress. Social support is a major determinant of successful coping. It comes as no surprise that the loss of a loved one ranks as one of the most stressful events in life.

The degree to which we need to control a situation impacts our perception about stressful life events. The most stressful events, according to research, are the ones in which we feel helpless.[150] For example, in the case of the patient Emma, having an alcoholic mother throughout her childhood was very traumatic. The patient remembered many episodes when she felt helpless and left alone to deal with problems a parent usually handles. One night, she awoke from a nightmare and went to her basement to look for her mother, whom she found passed out on the floor. Emma was only six years old and felt helpless to know what to do, both for herself and for her mother. She lay down on the floor next to her mother, waiting for her to wake up. The memory of this situation stayed with her into adulthood.

The more we feel empowered in our ability to deal with stressful situations, the more successful we can be. This does not apply to the pathological desires to control that are often seen in eating disorder patients. For them, any loss of control is actually extremely stressful and can trigger an increase in the eating disorder behaviors.

More recently, attention has also been directed to examination of an additional reaction to the fight/flight response to stress: the immobility or "freeze" response as noted by Peter Levine who describes this frozen state as one in which the "rage, terror and helplessness have built up to a level of activation that overwhelms the nervous system. At this point, immobility will take over and the individual will either freeze or collapse. What happens then is that the intense, frozen energy, instead of discharging, gets bound up with the overwhelming, highly activated, emotional states of terror, rage and helplessness."[151]

CASE EXAMPLE:

Joanie was raped at age nineteen in college. She was at a party and went to the bathroom. During her absence, her rapist put a drug in her drink that sedated and disoriented her. She doesn't remember leaving the party or even the rape itself. She woke up lying next to a man she'd spoken to briefly at the party. There was blood on the sheet all around her. The man woke up and began trying to have sex with her again. At that point, she froze out of fear and confusion and stopped fighting him. Later, when he fell back asleep, she got dressed and called a friend to pick her up. She blamed herself for not leaving sooner. What she didn't realize was that she had "frozen"—become numb in response to her fear and confusion. She couldn't have responded rationally in this state. She didn't tell anyone about the rape until two years later. Her experience illustrates how the frozen energy of the trauma becomes entangled with her fear, anger and helplessness, making it difficult for her to process the individual emotions of the trauma.

The immediate physiological reactions of the stress response include increased nervous system activation and the release of adrenaline and/or noradrenaline by the adrenal medulla. Adrenaline causes an increase in heart rate and blood pressure; shunting of blood flow from the skin (making persons in shock appear white or pale) and the digestive tract (which explains stomach upset during stress including nausea, vomiting, diarrhea, abdominal pain) to the muscles; dilation of pupils; and inhibition of tear glands and salivation (leading to the symptom of dry mouth). There is also mobilization of energy stored in the liver in the form of glycogen that is released into the bloodstream as glucose (thereby increasing blood sugar levels). All of these reactions prepare the body for the fight/flight response.

If the stress is very intense or becomes chronic, cortisol is released from the adrenal cortex into the bloodstream. Cortisol release has a normal diurnal variation: it is highest in the morning and lowest in the evening. Changes in cortisol levels in the blood have been observed in persons with depression and psychological stress. Physical stressors such as low blood sugar, illness, trauma, fever, emotional states, surgery, physical exercise, or extremes of temperature can also trigger cortisol release. Cortisol affects our immune system response, explaining the tendency of persons under stress to have more frequent colds and other illnesses. Chronic exposure to cortisol can cause elevated blood sugar, suppression of the inflammatory response, and slowing of bone formation (leading to loss of bone mass). These same symptoms are seen with chronic administration of prescription steroids used for asthma and other diseases and to suppress the immune system in transplant patients to avoid rejection of the transplanted organ.

The primitive fight or flight response allowed our ancient ancestors to respond to actual threats to their lives. Our nervous system is hardwired to respond to any perceived threat or stressor in this way even if the situation does not call for it. Posttraumatic stress disorder exemplifies this state of chronic activation and hypervigilance to memories or flashbacks of traumatic events that keep the nervous system on red alert. This chronic level of activation causes wear and tear on the body and can contribute to the development of various illnesses.

CASE EXAMPLE

Myra presented looking like a deer caught in the headlights. When the telephone rang in her therapist's office, she jumped noticeably. She appeared hypersensitive to any sound coming from outside the office and at one point, complained that "the birds near your office are really noisy." She had difficulty sleeping because her roommate made noises that frightened her. Her drug-addicted mother neglected her in childhood. Myra's younger life had been very chaotic with multiple moves to different houses. She lived in neighborhoods where she frequently witnessed violence outside her home. At the age of fifteen, two of her close friends had died— one by suicide, the other in a car accident. Jumpy, always expecting the worst to happen, she was an example of the hypervigilance caused by childhood trauma.

The Physiology of Stress

Another major player in the stress response is the hypothalamic-pituitary-adrenal (HPA) Axis, whose job it is to balance production of adrenaline from the adrenal medulla and corticosteroid production being released by the adrenal cortex. The hypothalamus and pituitary glands sit in the bony cavity called the sella turcica at the base of the brain. The hypothalamus links the nervous and endocrine systems via the pituitary gland, also known as the "master gland." The hypothalamus produces and secretes neurohormones that signal the release of certain hormones from the anterior pituitary gland:

- the growth hormone prolactin for production of breast milk;
- the gonadotropic hormones that control the growth and reproductive capacity of the gonads or sex organs, including the follicle-stimulating hormone (FSH), luteinizing hormone (LH), and luteotropic hormone;
- the thyroid stimulating hormone (TSH);
- adrenocorticotropic hormone (ACTH);
- endorphin;
- and other hormones.

The posterior pituitary produces oxytocin, which aids in the release of milk from the mammary glands and causes uterine contractions and antidiuretic hormone (ADH) (the water-conserving hormone).

Hypothalamus → Pituitary --→ Target Organ		
Thyrotropin releasing hormone TRH	Thyroid stimulating hormone (TSH)	Thyroid hormone (T3 and T4) from thyroid gland
Corticotropin-Releasing hormone (CRH)	ACTH and Beta-endorphins	Cortisol from adrenal glands
Gonadotropin releasing hormone (GnRH or LHRH)	Follicle stimulating hormone and Luetinizing hormone (FSH and LH)	Sex hormone release from ovaries, testes (estrogen, testosterone, progesterone)
Somatostatin or growth hormone-inhibiting hormone	Inhibits secretion of growth hormone	Liver and adipose (fat) tissue
Dopamine or prolactin-inhibiting hormone	Inhibits prolactin secretion	Ovaries, mammary glands

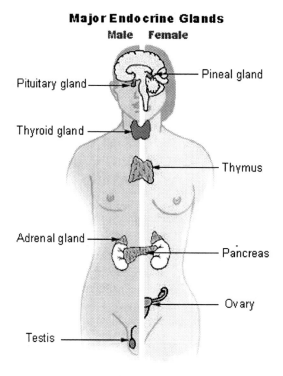

Major Endocrine Glands
Male   Female

Pituitary gland

Pineal gland

Thyroid gland

Thymus

Adrenal gland

Pancreas

Ovary

Testis

The control or release of these hormones is a negative feedback loop. As the hormone levels in the bloodstream increase, the hypothalamus produces less of the releasing hormones. The pituitary gland controls growth, blood pressure, some aspects of pregnancy and childbirth, breast milk production, sex organ function in men and women, thyroid gland function, the metabolism of food into energy, and the regulation of water retention and osmolarity in the body. The hypothalamus is a complex region that controls many functions in the body and is responsive to light for circadian and seasonal rhythms; smells, including pheromones; steroids; information from the heart, stomach, and reproductive tract; level of various hormones in the bloodstream; infecting bacteria or viruses; and stress. Stress in early life (such as would be present in childhood trauma) determines the ability of the *adult* hypothalamus to respond to stress. Appetite is one of the many bodily functions controlled in part by the hypothalamus. In reaction to stress, CRH is also secreted by the amygdala (involved in the processing and memory of emotional reactions). CRH secretion by the hypothalamus is probably most sensitive to physiological stress whereas secretion of CRH from the amygdala is more reactive to psychological stress.[152] HPA activity is increased in mood disorders such as anxiety, melancholic depression, and bipolar disorder.

Chronic cortisol excess leads to excessive fear, increased atherosclerosis through insulin resistance and visceral fat deposition, osteoporosis, and decreased immune function. Furthermore, one animal study found that the mesolimbic dopaminergic system is suppressed by hypercortisolemia (high blood levels of cortisol). If confirmed, this preliminary finding would allow researchers to make a link between HPA Axis overactivity and an impaired reward system, possibly correlated to the anhedonia (lack of pleasure experience), which is a core feature of major depression." It is possible that the HPA Axis dysfunction actually leads to MDD in anorexic patients."[153] In a study on major depressive disorder, Claes noted "…early adverse experience can produce a lasting effect on HPA Axis regulation as well, probably leading to a lifelong tendency to develop chronic CRH hyperdrive in response to stress. This has been shown in a number of animal studies, and recently some data in humans with early trauma have become available as well."[154]

In a study by Putignano et al., salivary and blood levels of cortisol were measured in anorexic, obese, and normal weight women. Anorexics in treatment and those who were newly diagnosed showed increased plasma and salivary levels of cortisol (although slightly lower in those in treatment). Decreased diurnal variations in cortisol were seen in both anorexics and obese patients compared with controls. Depression and anxiety scores were not related to cortisol levels.[155]

In a study of the psychoneuroendocrine characteristics of overweight and obese women, those women whose parents were obese were found to have a distinctive personality profile on the MMPI (Minnesota Multiphasic Personality Inventory) and higher release of ACTH in response to administration of corticotrophin-releasing hormone. The authors postulated that *HPA reactivity was a sensitive index for clinical psychological and possibly neural factors contributing to overweight and obesity* (italics added).[156]

Treatment with the antidepressant mirtazapine (Remeron) has been shown to inhibit cortisol concentrations in both healthy and depressed patients. A study testing the clinical effectiveness of using mirtazapine in treating anorexics demonstrated a trend toward increasing body mass index (BMI) and a significant inhibition of salivary cortisol levels over a three-week period. There was no difference in 21-HAM-D scores. It was unclear whether the medication was the cause of this attenuation of HPA Axis activity versus the onset of treatment including meal monitoring and cessation of purging.[157]

A study that compared physiological measures of stress as measured by salivary cortisol levels found a lack of congruence between participants' self-report of anxiety in an induced stressful situation and salivary cortisol levels during psychosocial stress.[158]

A recent small study found that compared with matched control patients, bulimics had decreases in the normal level of cortisol at 6 am and 2 pm and that in response to a stimulation challenge with corticotrophin releasing hormone, bulimics had a much higher release of ACTH (hyperactive HPA Axis) and cortisol (although cortisol results did not reach statistical significance). The conclusion was that bulimics may have a complex and poorly understood dysregulation of the HPA Axis associated with the disease.[159]

A study in patients with night eating syndrome (considered

part of ED-NOS) also demonstrated dysregulation of the HPA Axis with blunting of the CRH-induced ACTH and cortisol response.[160]

Stress Coping Styles in Eating Disorders

In a study of stress and coping mechanisms, women with eating disorders tended to avoid thinking about stressful situations or to ruminate about them. Bulimics in the study were more likely to be self-blaming and less likely to seek support from others. In general, the women in this study were less effective in coping with stressful situations than women without eating disorders.[161]

Soukup[162] studied coping styles of inpatient eating disorder patients and found that both anorexics and bulimics had higher levels of reported stress and less confidence in their ability to solve problems. They also showed a tendency to avoid facing their problems and expressed difficulty in sharing personal problems. Another study on coping strategies in eating disorder patients used the Ways of Coping Checklist to indicate how they dealt with stressors. Again, avoidance was found to be the primary coping mechanism. Bulimics and anorexics used more wishful thinking and asked for less social support than controls. Depression scores (Beck Depression Inventory) were higher in those using avoidant coping and lower in those patients who used problem-focused coping and seeking social support. This study concluded that "a treatment approach that teaches coping strategies, as well as removing the obstacles (cognitive, emotional, or practical) that preclude the use of more effective coping, may be a useful component of treatment."[163]

The link between depression and body image in bulimics is important as demonstrated by Keel's 2001 study showing that depression may be a better indicator of body dissatisfaction than bulimic symptoms.[164]

Stress, Mood Disorders, and Addictions

Drugs of abuse (DOAs) activate the corticotrophin-releasing factor (CRF)/HPA Axis during both use and withdrawal. While dopamine (DA) activity in the part of the brain called the nucleus accumbens is implicated in the reinforcement of all DOAs, CRF and noradrenaline (norepinephrine) pathways are involved in the stress-induced reinstatement of drug-seeking behavior in animals that are drug dependent. In drug addicts with or without comorbid depression, there is a decrease in the body's ability to respond to stress as evidenced by a decreased production of ACTH and cortisol in response to CRF compared with normal controls. This blunted cortisol response to psychological stress is also found in former smokers, alcoholics, and persons with polysubstance dependence and may be a marker for the same hyperactivity of the HPA Axis found in eating disorders. Stress is also one of the causes for relapse from SUD. Relapse from both cocaine[165] and nicotine[166] has been predicted in research studies by stress-induced drug craving.

Stress and PTSD

Stress also affects the incidence of PTSD and its connection to SUD. Substance users are more likely to be exposed to trauma and therefore have increased likelihood of developing PTSD compared with the general population. Persons suffering from trauma may use substances to self-medicate, which can lead to more symptoms associated with their PTSD and a more prolonged healing course. Studies in patients diagnosed with PTSD show hyperactive central CRH production. But as opposed to patients with major depressive disorder, the HPA Axis negative feedback is enhanced, resulting in a low production of cortisol.

A history of childhood abuse is associated with HPA Axis

hyperactivity, especially in women with current major depression who have a sixfold increase in ACTH release in response to stress. MRI scans of women with major depression who had been severely physically or sexually abused in childhood seem to indicate changes in brain structure in the limbic system and a permanent hyperactive stress response.[167]. Similar findings are seen in patients with borderline personality disorder (BPD) who have been abused and those diagnosed with PTSD who show increased pituitary ACTH production.

The HPA Axis, brain CRF, and the noradrenergic systems are all integrally involved in the stress response as well as in PTSD and SUD. There is a higher level of brain CRF in alcoholics going through withdrawal, with PTSD, and during withdrawal from cocaine. This increased brain CRF, especially in the emotional center of the brain called the amygdala, is the source of fear leading to hyperarousal or hypervigilance that can lead to higher risk of SUD and is associated with PTSD. Noradrenaline is increased in both alcohol and opioid withdrawal and can explain, in part, the higher incidence of PTSD symptoms during withdrawal from these substances.

CRF is also implicated in the development of anxiety and affective disorders. The comorbidity in epidemiological studies of major depression with nicotine, alcoholism, and other SUD varies from 32 to 54 percent. The connection between stress and negative affective states is well documented, and both are associated with increased drug craving in addicts. Chronic SUD can lead to dysregulation of the brain's reward systems and increase symptoms of major depression.

As with eating disorders, early life stress and/or chronic stress can lead to long-term changes in the body's ability to adapt to stress. Changes in the brain affect both the stress response and the reward pathway and may predispose to a vulnerability to substance use disorders or other psychiatric disorders or both.[168]

There are similar connections between stress and eating behaviors. Stress is the most common trigger for binge eating.

Under high stress, overeaters increase their intake of food more than those without a history of obesity. The ability to control weight is related to the tendency to overeat under stressful conditions. So-called high reactors to stress tend to eat more calories and eat foods that are higher in fat. In an animal model, "comfort foods" tend to blunt the acute stress response.[169] In a study by Dallman et al.,[170] women under high stress had increased food intake in response to emotional cues and tended to have higher visceral fat. The theory is that overeating is one of many adaptations to high stress. There appear to be overlapping brain circuits that regulate drug addiction and the drive to eat comfort foods. Patients with a history of overeating were given Naltrexone, an opiate antagonist, which resulted in a 33 percent decreased hunger for comfort foods compared with a 21 percent decrease in comfort foods in normal weight persons. The review concludes that the "present data suggests a single opioid mechanism is unlikely to explain all aspects of ingestive behavior, but also that opioid-mediated reward mechanisms play an important control in hedonic aspects of ingestion."[171]

In binge eating disorder (BED), the HPA Axis is hyperactive with high levels of cortisol that correlate to increased food intake and increased central body fat.[172]

The role of stress in the development and maintenance of eating disorders is increasingly well supported in research, providing another rationale and benefit for the use of complementary and alternative therapies in the treatment of eating disorders.

CHAPTER 8
USING HERBS TO COPE WITH STRESS

"What makes me so certain that the natural human lifespan is far in excess of the actual one is this. Among all my autopsies (and I have performed over 1,000), I have never seen a person who died of old age. In fact, I do not think that anyone has ever died of old age. We invariably die because one vital part has worn out too early in proportion to the rest of the body."
Dr. Hans Selye (one of the first to describe and research the stress response in the 1950s)

Stress is unavoidable and yet none of us is taught how to cope with stress. Developing adequate and healthy responses to stressful situations is helped by using an array of coping strategies. Herbs such as the adaptogens are a valuable component of a stress management approach.

Stress and the Adaptogens

Adaptogens are a category of herbal remedies that help the body adapt to stress, restoring homeostasis or balance and providing support to the adrenal glands. A 1968 paper by Soviet pharmacologists defined adaptogens this way:
- An adaptogen causes minimal change in the normal

physiologic functioning of the organism.

- The actions of adaptogens are nonspecific, i.e., they help the body resist or deal with a <u>wide range</u> of physical, chemical, and biological stressors.
- An adaptogen normalizes or balances physiologic processes (if a parameter is too high, the adaptogen will lower it and vice versa).

The term "adaptogen" was coined by Soviet scientists to describe herbs that increase resistance to illness and enhance vitality. Panax (Korean) ginseng, Siberian ginseng, astragalus, and Rhodiola rosea are examples of adaptogens thought to increase nonspecific resistance to physical, chemical, psychological, and biological stressors.

Ginseng includes several species listed under the genus *Panax* including Asian ginseng, Korean ginseng and American ginseng, but does not include *Siberian ginseng or Eleutherococcus senticosus,* which has been fostered in Russia as a cheaper alternative to ginseng. Panax ginseng as opposed to Siberian ginseng contains *ginsenosides* which are thought to be the active ingredients.

Ginseng root has been used in China for over two thousand years and are important herbs in traditional Chinese medicine (TCM). There is good scientific evidence for its use as a mental performance enhancer and in the treatment of noninsulin dependent (Type 2) diabetes mellitus (NIDDM). At doses of 200-400 mg of the standardized extract G115, ginseng has been shown in several studies to enhance thinking and learning, reaction time, concentration, and the ability to perform math and logic in both young, healthy subjects and in older, ill patients. A small number of human studies show that ginseng may lower blood sugar levels in NIDDM in the fasting state and after meals. Ginseng extract is often standardized to 4 percent ginsenosides (as found in G115) or 7 percent total ginsenosides. Tests of many over-the-counter products have shown that many do not contain what they claim and some may test positive for pesticides. Use of a well-known company is safest.[173]

Dosage
100-200 mg of the standardized Panax ginseng extract once or twice daily for up to twelve weeks. There is not enough evidence to recommend use in those under eighteen years of age.

Toxicity
Ginseng products are used by more than six million people annually in the United States alone and have an established safety profile. There is a report of a "ginseng abuse syndrome" in which ingestion of large doses of the root (greater than 3 g/day) improved motor and cognitive function but also resulted in skin rashes, diarrhea, anxiety, and insomnia. The concomitant use of caffeine during this study confounded the results. Ginseng has also been reported to have some estrogenlike qualities leading to breast tenderness and the formation of breast nodules as well as one case of vaginal bleeding in a seventy-two-year-old woman. The most common side effect is nervousness and excitation, which diminished over several days. It should be used with caution in diabetics due to the blood sugar-lowering effect. It should not be used in combination with MAO Inhibitors (Nardil, Parnate, Marplan) as it may cause mania. It may alter the effects of blood pressure or heart medication. Caution should be used when taking ginseng in combination with Lasix and Lanoxin. Tinctures of ginseng contain alcohol and should not be used by those with alcohol abuse history or who are taking Antabuse or other drugs (Flagyl) that react to alcohol.

Siberian ginseng (*Eleutherococcus senticosus*) has primarily been studied in Russia and largely ignored in Chinese medicine. The root is the part of this flowering shrub that is used medicinally. Siberian ginseng does not contain ginsenosides but shares many of the chemical constituents of P. ginseng. In animal studies, Siberian ginseng increased sleep latency and duration when given with hexobarbital (a sedative). In humans, injecting Siberian ginseng increased the activity of the immune system, increasing absolute T-cell count. Other studies done in Russia included the following findings:

1. a reduction of 20 to 30 percent in total disease incidents in a study of 1,200 drivers at an auto plant given 8-12 mg of SG daily for two months.
2. a reduction of influenza and acute respiratory disease in a group of 180 men given 0.5 ml every day of SG tincture and compared with a control group. Influenza and acute respiratory disease decreased from 17 percent in the previous time frame to 12.7 percent.
3. a reduction of high blood pressure and ischemic heart disease in 1,200 drivers at an auto plant. There were 3.5 times fewer cases of high blood pressure; ischemic heart disease dropped from 6.7 per 100 workers to 0.2 per 100 workers. Lost days at work decreased from 282 to 3.
4. possible use in surgical patients to improve postoperative recovery.
5. possible use for reduction in toxic side effects of medications used to treat cancer and in environmental toxins such as insecticides.

Other purported uses for Siberian ginseng include improvement in vision, diabetes, chronic gastritis, atherosclerosis, brain injuries, tuberculosis, and neurasthenia. (Neurasthenia is an ill-defined medical condition characterized by lassitude, fatigue, headache, and irritability and is associated chiefly with emotional disturbance).[174]

Rhodiola rosea is also known as "golden root" and "roseroot" and grows at high altitudes in Arctic areas of Europe and Asia. The Greek physician Dioscorides recorded its use in 77 B.C.E. Rhodiola has been used for centuries in traditional medicine in Russia and other countries. It also was used in the twentieth century by Russian cosmonauts. More than 180 studies have been done on Rhodiola since 1960.

Traditional medicine uses include increasing physical endurance, work productivity, longevity, and resistance to altitude sickness and treating fatigue, depression, nervous system disorders, impotence, and gastrointestinal disorders. Its properties as an adaptogen have been well documented for protecting animals and humans from mental and physical stress, toxic exposures, and cold. Rhodiola rosea extracts used in clinical studies were generally standardized to 3 percent rosavins and 0.8-1 percent salidroside to approximate the naturally occurring ratio of these two active compounds in Rhodiola.

The Pharmacological and Pharmacopoeia Committee of the Soviet Ministry of Health recommends R. rosea as a general health tonic, for somatic and infectious illnesses, in psychiatric and neurological conditions, and in healthy persons to treat fatigue and increase attention span, memory, and productivity at work. In Sweden, R. Rosea is considered to be an antifatigue agent and is used to increase mental work capacity during stress, as a general "strengthener" and as a psychostimulant.

R. rosea has effects on many different neuronal pathways promoting the release of norepinephrine, 5-hydroxytryptamine and dopamine. It also works as an antioxidant, helping to protect the nervous system from damage of free radicals. This function helps fight the effects of stress that interfere with memory functions and over time, cause deterioration in memory function. The positive benefits of R. rosea on memory and cognitive function may be due to the dual action of stimulating cognition and calming emotions.

As a psychostimulant, R. rosea was shown to be effective in a study of 412 patients with neuroses and asthenic syndromes (fatigue, decrease in work productivity, difficulty falling asleep, loss of appetite, irritability, and headaches). When compared with fifty-three controls, R. rosea improved symptoms at a dose of 50 mg three times daily.

R. rosea should not be used in patients with mania as it does not reduce manic symptoms and could worsen paranoid states. However, in schizophrenic patients whose medications have caused Parkinson's-like symptoms, R. rosea was found to be beneficial.

Stress has an effect on brain neurotransmitter levels. Serotonin is integrally involved in the body's response to stress and many stressors cause decreased levels of serotonin in the hypothalamus. R. rosea may work by increasing serotonin in the hypothalamus and midbrain. It also reduces the activation of other parts of the stress response. In animal models, R. rosea modulated the release of beta-endorphins, preventing excess release during stress. It has also been shown to modulate release of opioid peptides, corticotrophin releasing factor (CRF) and catecholamines (norepinephrine and epinephrine) thereby improving stress tolerance. R. rosea has also been shown to enhance the function of the thyroid and adrenal glands.

Adaptogens can be useful in the treatment of eating disorders by serving to modulate the hyperactivity of the HPA Axis both acutely by its action of modulating release of catecholamines and chronically by its effect on CRF. R. rosea can also serve as an adjunct treatment to comorbid depression, anxiety, and fatigue. Interestingly, in a study of forty women with amenorrhea (loss of menstrual cycles) who took 100 mg R. rosea extract twice a day for two weeks, twenty-five had return of normal menses and eleven became pregnant. While this study was not done in women specifically with eating disorders, there is no reason to doubt that R. rosea could be of help in this population with amenorrhea. It has been shown to improve sexual function in men as well.

 Toxicity and Side Effects
At the usual clinical doses of 200-600 mg/day, R. rosea is considered very safe. Side effects in those

who have anxiety could include increased activation, jitteriness, or agitation. If this occurs, reducing the dosage will alleviate the symptoms. It should be taken early in the day to avoid interfering with sleep. It should not be used in bipolar patients due to a theoretical possibility of inducing mania. There are no reports of R. rosea interacting with other medications, but it may be additive to stimulants. It should be taken on an empty stomach for best absorption. [175]

CASE EXAMPLE:

Meg was a twenty-year-old white female with a history of polysubstance dependence beginning with Ritalin and escalating to cocaine and then heroin by age seventeen. For the previous three years, Meg was in and out of treatment facilities. She provided a history of bulimia that predated her drug use and admitted to using drugs to help control her fear of gaining weight. Meg also gave a history of depression that may have been substance related. She had been tried on numerous prescription antidepressants and mood stabilizers with minimal benefit. At the time of her admission, she was taking Lexapro and Lamictal at maximum dosages. Meg's depression was vegetative with complaints of fatigue and hopelessness. She expressed chronic suicidal thoughts without intent or plan. Her Beck Hopelessness Scale (BHS) showed a high level of hopelessness. Over the course of her treatment, she was put on omega-3 fatty acids and 5-HTP to support her mood without marked changes in her level of depression. She was continued on her prescription medications. In addition to these, she was placed on R. rosea at a starting dose of 200 mg twice daily, which was increased to 400 mg twice daily without any adverse side effects. After approximately four weeks on this regimen, the patient expressed an improved, stabler mood and less fatigue. Her Beck Depression Inventory at discharge showed a minimal level of depression. She was continued on this regimen for one year with continued mood stability. Despite one relapse, she was able to maintain a two-year period of sobriety for the first time in three years through a combination of ongoing outpatient treatment and a supportive sober living environment.

Astragalus (*Astragalus membranaceus*) has been used since ancient times in Traditional Chinese medicine (TCM). It is a stimulant of the immune system (in lab and animal studies), stimulating the pituitary-adrenal cortical activity and supporting production of red blood cells in bone marrow. The root is the active part of the plant. Most of the research supporting the traditional medicine uses of astragalus is unclear. However, this herb has been used for thousands of years in TCM for the following indications:

1. Antiviral activity: reported in laboratory and animal studies. There is limited research in humans, and most has included combinations of astragalus with the drug interferon or with other herbs. Most studies were small and poorly designed.

2. Cancer: early laboratory and animal studies reported increases in immune cell function and decreases in cancer cell growth. Studies in humans are lacking.

3. Other uses: treatment of heart failure, immune system stimulation, liver protection (from damage related to toxins or Hepatitis B and C), heart infections (myocarditis/endocarditis), kidney failure, and upper respiratory tract infections. It also has been used to reduce chemotherapy side effects, but no good studies support this.

Drug-Herb interactions:
Astragalus may decrease blood sugar levels. Caution is advised in diabetics. At doses below 15 g, astragalus may lower blood pressure; at higher levels, it may raise blood pressure. Astragalus may increase the risk of bleeding when taken

with other medications or herbs that affect bleeding time. It may act as a diuretic and could theoretically lead to dehydration. Astragalus may reduce the effectiveness of sedatives such as Phenobarbital or hypnotic agents and increase the effects of drugs such as colchicines, succinylcholine, or pancuronium; stimulants such as ephedrine or epinephrine; haldol; and the cancer drug procarbazine.[176]

CASE EXAMPLE:

Becca is a twenty-nine-year-old engineering student who presented for treatment of anorexia nervosa at 74 percent of IBW. She was petite with a thin frame, pale skin, and a frail appearance. She wore baggy overalls and quickly demonstrated a penchant for arguing that supported her enmeshment with her disease. Because she wanted proof to justify any supplement use, laboratory testing was ordered. The results showed deficiency in zinc, antioxidants, and calcium. Becca had a bone density scan showing osteopenia/borderline osteoporosis. Her blood pressure was low normal at 90/50. Routine labs showed anemia (low iron). She was started on calcium and magnesium for bone support and zinc citrate 60 mg twice daily for two months to stimulate appetite and enhance weight gain and treat the zinc deficiency. Her multivitamin included an adequate amount of antioxidants and iron. Becca was given 1 gram twice daily of omega-3 fatty acids to improve the metabolism of zinc. Her weight gain was slow and the patient was diagnosed on evaluation and testing to have major depression. She was persuaded to try astragalus at a dose of 500 mg twice daily of root capsules for anemia and as an adaptogen. Within two weeks, her complexion appeared rosier and she expressed increased appetite and energy levels. Her blood pressure also increased to a more normal 110/70. Becca reported that she felt less tired and that her thinking was clearer. Over the following months, her anemia resolved.

Summary

From an integrative medicine perspective, it is important to support the body's self-healing capacity rather than to simply treat symptoms. Components can include nutrition, healthy exercise, digestive support, and sleep restoration as well as stress reduction. Adaptogens are a class of herbs that can be used to support the body's ability to deal with the stress of chronic debilitating illnesses such as eating disorders and reduce the hyperactive HPA Axis response to stressors of all types. In addition, adaptogens can promote mental clarity, support mood and energy, and improve immune functioning during the recovery phase. Given the low side effect profile and minimal interaction with other medications, their use should be encouraged in patients with eating disorders.

CASE EXAMPLE: More about Tara:

Tara's psychological testing showed that she met DSM-IV criteria for PTSD. She continued to have flashbacks and nightmares about 9/11 and sadness about those who had died. Her moods were stabler; however, she complained of a continued lack of pleasure in her usual activities as well as low energy. An attempt to increase the dosage of her antidepressant medication resulted in reports of increased sedation. The dose was lowered to its original amount and Tara was started on R. rosea at a dosage of 50 mg twice daily. She reported improvement in her energy level over the first week of treatment. Her flat moods improved only minimally. The R. rosea was increased over the following week to 100 mg twice daily at which point Tara reported feeling more alert. She reported that while participating in the climbing wall activity with her group, she felt happy for the first time in a long time. In her therapeutic grief process group, Tara was able to symbolically say good-bye to the friends she'd lost in 9/11 and to create her own tribute to them—a drawing of a tree growing from ground zero with the faces of her friends on the branches. In guided imagery, Tara was able to describe pain in her chest. When imaging the "space" of the pain, she described a red-hot area shaped like a dagger. She also described a constriction in her throat, described as an "anvil stuck in my throat." Tara was able to identify the red, hot cylinder in her chest as anger at her rapist that she had turned on herself, blaming herself for not being more careful and somehow not avoiding being raped. The anvil in her throat represented the loss of her voice going back to childhood when she was in gymnastics and was exacerbated by the rape, which she kept secret. She envisioned being able to slowly pry the anvil from her throat and to see the cylinder cooling and shrinking. She painted both images and used them as targets in her EMDR and Somatic work.

CHAPTER 9
THE ENERGY OF HEALING – EXPLORING MIND-BODY THERAPIES

Confusion is an ally of your disease. If you stop and look you may find that the distraction of confusion allows you to avoid the real issues at the root of your distress.
Carolyn Ross, MD

The energy of healing: an overview of CAM therapies with research evidence that supports their efficacy and examples of their use in practice.

What is the energy of healing? As patients go through their healing process in treatment, there are changes that become noticeable in their physical appearance. The obvious ones have to do with the results of refeeding in which patients lose or gain weight, their complexions improve, their eyes appear brighter. Along with these physical changes are the changes in the subtle energy body. For example, acupuncturists, who diagnose medical illness based on the patterns of flow in the body's energy channels, can often diagnose patterns of chemical dependency or depression based on these patterns of energy. Likewise, any experienced clinician will notice that patients may appear "clearer, less shut down or more open and at peace." All of these changes have their correlates in the body's vital energy. Why? Because whatever affects the mind (cognitive therapy, emotional release, etc.) also affects the body. This is the simplest premise of mind-body medicine.

The techniques in mind-body medicine (MBM) are the same ones that spurred the development of psychotherapy, beginning with hypnosis and guided imagery. Given the intersection between stress, addictions, and eating disorders, mind-body therapies are critical in the treatment of these co-occurring conditions. The benefits of MBM are linked to the neuroendocrine effects of the **stress reaction** (fight versus flight versus freeze) and their role in illness. **Current research suggests that reversal or attenuation of the stress response may play a role in the treatment and prevention of disease.** As this relates to psychiatric diagnoses, current advances in technology such as topographic EEG mapping and spectral analysis have enabled researchers to document that **by changing mental activity, one can also change central nervous system activity.** Mindfulness and the therapies that support mindfulness are important tools in the management of eating disorders for a number of reasons.

Mind-Body Therapies in Eating Disorders

In every ancient tradition, there are sacred rituals and ceremonies that surround food and eating. In traditions such as Ayurveda and traditional Chinese medicine, those who serve as guides or healers hold a sacred place for food and nutrition in their prescriptions for health. In our current fast-paced culture, the sacredness of food is often lost. Modern-day rituals for many do not include sitting at a meal together and sharing food mindfully, but rather center on the family driving through a fast-food takeout restaurant and eating in their cars on the way to soccer practice or other activities. The fact that Americans eat so many meals in their cars has complicated Japanese automakers' design of vehicles to be sold in the United States;

maintenance of cars that also serve as dinner tables is more difficult.

Prayers before eating are one way to focus ourselves mindfully before eating. One example of such a prayer is from the Buddhist tradition which is used in a silent meal:

1. **Looking at Your Empty Plate or Bowl**
   My plate (bowl), empty now,
   will soon be filled with precious food.

2. **Serving Food**
   In this food I see clearly
   the presence of the entire universe
   supporting my existence.

3. **Sitting Down**
   Sitting here is like sitting under the Bodhi Tree.
   My body is mindfulness itself,
   calm and at ease,
   free from distraction.

4. **Looking at the Plate of Food before Eating**
   Beings all over the Earth
   are struggling to live.
   May we practice
   so that all may have enough to eat.

5. **Contemplating the Food**
   This plate of food,
   so fragrant and appetizing,
   also contains much suffering.

6. **The Five Contemplations**
   (READ ALOUD BY ONE PERSON BEFORE
   BEGINNING TO EAT)
   This food is a gift of the earth, the sky, numerous living beings, and much hard work.
   May we eat with mindfulness and gratitude so as to be worthy to receive this food.
   May we recognize and transform unwholesome mental formations especially our greed.

May we take only foods that nourish us and prevent illness (and promote well-being).

We accept this food so that we may nurture our sisterhood and brotherhood, build our Sangha, and nourish our ideal of serving living beings.

7. **Beginning to Eat**
   (RECITED SILENTLY WHILE CHEWING THE FIRST FOUR MOUTHFULS)
   With the first mouthful, I practice the love that brings joy.
   With the second mouthful, I practice the love that relieves suffering.
   With the third mouthful, I practice the joy of being alive.
   With the fourth mouthful, I practice equal love for all beings.

8. **When the Plate/Bowl Is Empty**
   My plate (bowl) is empty.
   My hunger is satisfied.
   I am determined to live for the benefit of all beings.

9. **Drinking Tea**
   This cup of tea in my two hands,
   mindfulness is held uprightly.
   My body and mind dwell
   in the very here and now.

10. **Washing the Dishes**
    Washing the dishes is like bathing a baby Buddha.
    The profane is the sacred.
    Everyday mind is Buddha's mind.[177]

Research on Mind-Body Therapies in Eating Disorders

One study by Pop-Jordanova[178] on seventy-six obese, twenty-six AN, and thirty-five healthy girls showed that anorexia and hyperphagia (binge eating) are specifically stress related. In this study, Electrodermal Response (EDR) biofeedback was effective support for mitigation of ED behaviors. EDR biofeedback measures skin conductance, which is a way to measure sympathetic nervous system activation or the stress response.

Esplen et al.[179] found that one effective treatment for eating disorders was guided imagery. In a study of fifty women with bulimia who were randomized to receive six weeks of guided imagery or no treatment, women in the guided imagery cohort showed a 74 percent reduction in bingeing and 75 percent reduction in self-induced vomiting. This study also showed improvements in attitudes regarding eating, dieting, and body weight as well as self-reported loneliness and ability to practice self-comforting. Laessle[180] demonstrated a faster reduction in binge frequency in fifty-five female patients diagnosed with BN who were assigned to stress management or nutritional management. There were decreases in vomiting, body dissatisfaction, and depression. Stress management led to improvement in feelings of ineffectiveness, interpersonal distrust, and anxiety.

Hypnosis has been found to enhance the benefits of cognitive behavioral therapy in the treatment of phobia, obesity, and anxiety.[181]

CASE EXAMPLE:

Marla was admitted for the treatment of anorexia nervosa. She came from a wealthy family and was the oldest of three children. Her parents were married; her mother suffered from severe depression and had been hospitalized off and on throughout her childhood. During her mother's hospitalizations, Marla was in charge of her younger brother and sister. Marla described herself as a sad and shy child. She idolized and was afraid of her mother and described her relationship with her father as emotionally distant. Marla herself had been diagnosed with depression at the age of seventeen and feared that her life would turn out to be like her mother's. In a session of guided imagery, Marla was able to identify her depression as a hard, black ball that she felt in the center of her chest. She felt the ball was dense and hot with a red interior. In imagery, she was guided to go inside the ball and move around and was able to identify anger, sadness, and guilt as emotions inside this metaphoric representation of her depression. When asked to locate in memory the earliest time she felt this sadness, Marla remembered being seven years old. She had short hair and was wearing red cowboy boots, her favorite shoes. She was at home with her sister and her mother. She described feeling sad and fearful. Her mother had been in her room all day and Marla knew this meant her mother was "sick" again. Marla and her sister were hungry but didn't want to disturb their mother. Marla felt overwhelmed with responsibility for her sister but afraid of asking her mother for help. She was in a no-win situation and could see her younger self paralyzed with fear. Marla also was able to get in touch with anger at her mother for not being there for her. In treatment, Marla struggled with recurrent fears of being like her mother. If she felt appropriately sad, she would begin to worry that this meant her depression was worsening. Using breathing techniques and imagery, Marla was able to learn to calm some of her fears and reduce her levels of anxiety.

Mind-Body Therapies for Mental Health

Mind-body therapies (MBT) have also been shown to be effective in treating comorbidities of eating disorder patients as well as some of the symptoms that are troublesome for many patients.

Biofeedback and hypnosis have been successful in helping patient with insomnia. [182] Benson's work at the Harvard Mind

Body Institute has shown that the relaxation response meditation is effective in reducing cortisol levels as well as heart rate and blood pressure. Meditation also decreases stress-related symptoms including depression.[183] Three randomized comparative studies that examined treatment of moderate depression showed that relaxation therapy enhanced pharmacotherapy.[184]

In a *Journal of the American Medical Association* review on insomnia related to chronic pain, for example, biofeedback was cited as being helpful. A randomized trial of hypnosis found it helped patients get to sleep more quickly than placebo.[185]

Hypnosis produces a state of focused concentration without regard to surroundings and intrusive thoughts. Suggestions given during a hypnotic state can promote changes in thinking, behavior, or emotional release. In a review of the literature on depression, only anecdotal accounts and case reports were found. A 1995 meta-analysis of eighteen studies that included two on anxiety disorders and one on snake phobia compared a combination of cognitive-behavioral therapy (CBT) plus hypnosis with CBT alone. The clients in the combined group had greater improvements than at least 70 percent of clients not receiving hypnotherapy. It has been recommended that hypnosis be avoided in psychotic disorders as there is concern that latent psychosis may be activated.[186]

Applied relaxation (AR) or relaxation therapy (RT) includes many different techniques designed to achieve a generalized relaxation response. The results of seven small controlled studies using relaxation therapy for depression found it to be better than no treatment, as good as tricyclic antidepressants and cognitive behavior therapy, and less effective than exercise. When combined with medication, it was more effective than medication alone.[187]

In two research trials on generalized anxiety disorder (GAD), CBT and AR were both significantly successful, improving symptoms 50 to 60 percent.

Mindfulness meditation (MM), unlike other mind-body therapies (MBT) that originated in religious traditions or a spiritual context, encourages practitioners to observe their thoughts and perceptions without judgment on a moment-to-moment basis. The focus of meditative practice is on emptying the mind. In a study on MM used to treat anxiety and panic disorders, the participants demonstrated both subjective and objective decreases in anxiety and depression that was maintained at three-month and three-year follow-ups.[188] [189] Two researchers also suggested a possible role for MM or CBT in reducing relapse rates in depression.[190]

Progressive muscle relaxation (PMR) is a technique in which individual muscle groups are alternately tensed and relaxed. PMR was comparable to CBT in reducing symptoms in adolescents with depression from moderate levels of depression to a nondepressed state. There was also improvement in anxiety and academic self-concept.

Mindful Movement Therapies

Feldenkrais: In a study by Laumer et al. (1997), Feldenkrais produced increased body contentment, self-confidence, and general emotional maturation in fifteen eating disorder patients compared with fifteen controls.

About Yoga and Feldenkrais:

Feldenkrais uses techniques to facilitate learning about movement, posture, and breathing, thereby increasing range of motion and improving flexibility and coordination.

Yoga is a Sanskrit word meaning "to unite." There are many branches. Hatha yoga includes techniques to enhance concentration, breathing exercises, dietary guidelines and a series of exercises or poses also called asanas. The poses help bring the body into balance by slowing mental business, increasing flexibility, and massaging internal organs. Regular yoga practice helps reduce stress and bring a relaxed state into our daily lives.

Yoga and yogic breath work: While many of the studies on yoga have been done in India, most had small sample sizes and each used a different form of yoga practice, limiting generalizability. In a study on participants with mild depression, two one-hour iyengar yoga classes were compared with a wait list control group. Subjects in the yoga group demonstrated decreased depression and trait anxiety scores by self-report and decreased negative mood and fatigue after yoga class. There was a trend toward higher morning cortisol in the intervention group compared with the controls.[191]

Sudarshan kriya yoga (SKY) is a form of yogic breath work that involves rhythmic hyperventilation at differing rates of breathing. In one study, SKY[192] was compared with electroconvulsive therapy (ECT) and with imipramine in a sample of forty-five hospitalized patients with melancholic depression who had HAM-D scores of 17 or more. There were significant reductions in Beck Depression Inventory scores and HAM-D scores for depression in all groups. At the end of the study, remission rates were equivalent for yoga practice (67 percent) and imipramine (73 percent) and lower than remission rates for ECT (93 percent). These results may not be generalizable to an outpatient setting.

A similar study using yogic breathing techniques to treat obsessive-compulsive disorder (OCD) resulted in overall mean improvement on the Yale-Brown Obsessive Compulsive Scale of 54 percent for the five subjects completing the one-year program.[193] Hatha yoga has been shown to be effective in reducing drug use and criminal activity in patients on methadone maintenance[194] and other drug-addicted persons.[195]

Some view yoga as exercise, and so the question must be raised as to whether it is the benefit of any exercise that affects mood or if yoga is somehow different. Is mindfulness-based exercise as good as aerobics in enhancing mood? In a study by Netz et al.,[196] a single session of aerobic exercise (dance or swimming) was compared with one session of yoga or Feldenkrais. In this study, a computer class served as the control group. State anxiety scores and subjective well-being were lower in the Feldenkrais, yoga, and swimming groups when compared with aerobic dance or the control group. Self-reported depression was improved in all groups. Lack of benefit of aerobic exercise may have been confounded by the younger age of the participants. The commonalities between swimming, Feldenkrais, and yoga are in their lack of competitiveness, breath awareness, and repetitive movements, which may point to a shared mechanism of action.

Qigong and tai chi have been practiced in China as early as 2000 B.C.E. and are thought to be derived from yoga or Tibetan Buddhist martial arts practices. Qigong and one of its many forms, tai chi, are Chinese movement therapies based on the view that the causes of mental illness have to do with blockage of qi (vital energy) or accumulation of unexpressed emotions or "toxic energy" in the body. Qigong involves meditation, visualization, breathing, and movement.

The Qigong and Energy Medicine database[197] claims over 3,500 references. Of three double-blind studies on qigong for depression, only one yields significant positive benefit. Five studies examined the effect of qigong on treatment of anxiety, with only one showing promising evidence of therapeutic effect. One study found qigong to be effective in decreasing drug withdrawal symptoms, state anxiety, and sleep quality in heroin addicts compared with those receiving medication for detoxification or symptomatic care only.

One rare side effect of "erroneous" qigong may be the so-called "qigong-induced psychoses." This side effect may be more appropriately labeled "qigong-precipitated psychoses" in which the practice of qigong acts as a stressor in vulnerable individuals.

Patient comments about mind-body therapies:

- "The meditation class helped me to get back in touch

with my spiritual connection, something I'd lost after my last relapse."

- "When I practice the breathing exercises, I feel my breath moving into my belly and I experienced a difference between the 'flesh' of my belly which I'd worried about for so long (wanting a flat belly) and the gratitude I have for how my 'insides' all work together."
- "When I first started taking yoga, I was embarrassed and couldn't do most of the poses. After taking classes for a month, I was surprised at how flexible I really am.Yoga really helped build my self-confidence."

Energetic Therapies that foster the Mind-Body Connection

Zero balancing (ZB), designed to connect energy with structure, integrates Eastern principles of energy and healing with Western scientific investigation of human anatomy and quantum physics. The ZB technique was developed by Fritz Smith, MD, who states: "If you can balance something to neutral without judgment or comparison by holding it in its own space, it will naturally move to its highest possible benefit."[198]

ZB works at the interface of energy and structure and with expanded fields of consciousness. Not like other energy therapies, ZB does not "give" energy to patients. There are currently no research studies documenting the effectiveness of ZB.

Patient comments about ZB:
- "Zero balancing was life changing."
- "When I had my zero balancing treatment, I felt a wave of emotion well up in me and I cried throughout the treatment. I felt as if I'd left a lot of sadness on the table."

Reiki involves the transfer of energy through the practitioner to the patient to enhance the body's natural ability to heal itself through the balancing of energy. The mechanism for the effect of Reiki is poorly understood. A study to test potential biological and physiological mechanisms for Reiki found that biological markers related to stress reduction showed increase in salivary Immunoglobulin A (IgA) (associated with lowered stress response and decreased risk for infections), a significant drop in systolic blood pressure, decreases in skin temperature and muscle tension (not statistically significant), and a significant reduction in anxiety.[199]

Reiki also was shown to reduce pain and improve quality of life but not reduce opioid use in cancer patients receiving either opioids plus rest or opioids plus Reiki.[200] Reiki has been shown to reduce symptoms of psychological distress compared with control groups receiving "placebo" Reiki, with results continuing for one year after treatment ended.[201] Other energetic touch healing modalities such as Healing Touch and Johrei have shown similar benefits for drug addiction[202] and mood states.[203]

Patient comments about Reiki:
- "Reiki was a miracle."
- "Reiki calmed me and centered my emotions."
- "I was amazed by this process (Reiki) as a way to heal."

Bodywork Therapies

A study on CAM use by psychiatric inpatients showed that 21 percent used massage, chiropractic, acupuncture, and yoga for treatment of anxiety and depression as well as weight loss.[204]

Massage therapy decreases levels of cortisol (an average decrease of 31 percent) and increases serotonin (28 percent) and dopamine (31 percent).[205] One study of nineteen women with AN compared standard treatment alone to standard treatment with massage therapy twice per week for five weeks.

The massage group reported decreased stress and lower anxiety and had a decrease in cortisol levels after their massage treatment. The massage group also expressed decreases in body dissatisfaction (as measured by the Eating Disorder Inventory) and had increased dopamine and norepinephrine levels.[206]

A study in 24 inpatient bulimic adolescents showed those who received massage versus the control group who received standard treatment experienced decreases in self-reported and observed anxiety and depression. They had lower depression scores, lower cortisol (stress) levels, and higher dopamine levels and improved on several other psychological and behavioral measures.[207]

A review of research showed significant reductions in cortisol in patients with depression (including those with a history of sexual abuse and eating disorders), pain syndromes, autoimmune conditions (including asthma and chronic fatigue), HIV, and breast cancer and other studies looking at on the job stress, stress of aging and the stress of pregnancy. The results indicate a stress-alleviating effect and activating effect of massage therapy on a wide variety of conditions.[208]

Massage has also been shown to be effective in treating depression, comorbid in many ED patients, in a study in depressed teen mothers who received ten thirty-minute sessions of massage therapy or relaxation therapy over five weeks. Both groups reported lowered anxiety, but only the massage group showed stress hormone changes plus decreases in anxious behavior, pulse, and salivary cortisol.[209]

Patient comments about massage:
- "Massage was very helpful for my stress."
- "Massage really relaxed me and made a lot of things I was focused on go away."
- "(Massage was) much needed after a very tough EMDR."
- "Massage actually helped my program."

- "Massage was very spiritual and I find it vital to my recovery."

Chiropractic: Chiropractors represent the second largest group of primary care providers in the United States. Manipulative therapies have been part of healing therapies in almost all native cultures from the ancient Greeks to Native Americans. Chiropractic comes from the Greek *cheir* (hand) and *praxis* (practice). The founder of chiropractic medicine, Daniel D. Palmer, felt that "any disease process anywhere in the body is affected at least in part by the ability of the nervous system to enervate and enliven that area."[210]

Chiropractic manipulation was shown to have a beneficial effect on the stress response in one pilot study demonstrating decreases in salivary cortisol for at least one hour after treatment.

CASE EXAMPLE: More on Tara

Tara continued to progress. She found her meditation class very relaxing and expressed to the treatment team that she had never been able to meditate in the past due to her "racing thoughts." She was also enjoying yoga. She was no longer intellectualizing her issues but was now able to connect more easily to her emotions and the sensations in her body. Her negative thinking had decreased so that she had ED thoughts less than 50 percent of the time. Tara felt that massage had helped her to become more comfortable with her body and less obsessed with being judged by others. She found Reiki to be very relaxing and felt as if her body had more energy after Reiki treatments. She described the experience of one Reiki session by saying: "I felt like my body was 'waking up' and I felt a sensation of 'sparks' shooting through my body from my head to my feet." Her moods became somewhat more stable. However, during Tara's fourth week in treatment, her mother and father came for a four-day family week program. On the Sunday prior to family week, she had dinner with her parents for the first time since her admission. At dinner, her father expressed surprise that she was "eating so much." Her mother complimented Tara on how "healthy" she was looking. Tara immediately began to feel as if her cheeks were fat and felt like her abdomen was "huge and disgusting." After dinner, Tara had the urge to purge and sought the help of her therapist. She described her meal with her parents as "bringing back all my fear about gaining weight and being fat." When asked what she was feeling, Tara was tearfully able to connect her feelings to fear of being judged by her parents and fear that she was losing control, a feeling she'd experienced after 9/11. She was able to use some of the breathing techniques she'd learned to calm herself down. She felt more hopeful than she had in a long time. Tara completed family week and was able to express her anger at her mother for judgmental messages she'd received as a child. She expressed to her father the sadness she felt in not being closer to him. Tara was able to share with her parents her feelings of sadness and loss associated with her trauma. The ED team felt that a first step had been made toward healing. The staff remained concerned about the mother's ability to respect Tara's boundaries and both parents' willingness to support Tara as an adult, not a child under their control any longer.

CHAPTER 10
SEEING THINGS FROM A DIFFERENT PERSPECTIVE

"There are many roads to healing."
Carolyn Ross, MD from *Miracles in Healing*

This chapter provides a discussion of traditional systems of healing and their relevance to the treatment of eating disorders. The five-element acupuncture system, Ayurvedic medicine, and chakras are discussed in relation to their ability to share some of the patients' descriptions of their disease not easily explained in conventional medicine. Most patients with eating disorders measure their body image against prevailing Western cultural influences—movie stars, other famous people, models, and fashion icons. The purpose of this chapter is to provide alternative ways of thinking about body image and body size with the message: "Your body doesn't have to look a certain way."

Health and healing are defined in many different ways. The World Health Organization's definition is that "health is a state of complete physical, mental and social well-being and not merely the absence of disease or infirmity." Recently, this has been modified to include the ability to lead a "socially and economically productive life." There is argument about this definition from those who feel that health is not a state, rather a process requiring continuous adjustment.[211]

Conventional medicine tends to view health as a victory in the war against illness. We use terms that describe the "war machine" that is medicine: we wage war on AIDS, fight heart disease and try to eradicate cancer. Even the names of medications speak to medicine versus the disease: *anti*biotics, *anti*depressants and *anti*hypertensive drugs. We even wage war on aging. Conventional or allopathic medicine uses high-tech treatments in its war against illness.

Psychology defines healing as a process in the service of the evolution of the whole personality toward ever greater and more complex wholeness.* A nursing definition of healing is: the process of bringing together aspects of one's self, body-mind-spirit, at deeper levels of inner knowing, leading to integration and balance with each aspect having equal importance and value.α

How we define healing often relates to whether a certain treatment has been a success or a failure. In strict conventional medical terms, if a patient dies despite our best efforts to save him or her, we often view that as a failure. In spiritual terms, death can be defined as a different form of healing, even healing on the highest level.

The importance of scientific beliefs that have taken precedence in conventional medicine philosophy and training has had the effect of negating our understanding and belief in our natural capacity to heal and our place in and connection to the natural world. These shifts also stemmed from the seventeenth century philosopher, Descartes, whose concept of dualism influenced the belief that mind and body operated separately. Descartes led the charge toward this mechanistic view of man, which continues to influence medicine and

* From: Comfort A. On healing Americans. J Operational Psychiatry. 1978;9: 25-36.

α From: Jackson C. Healing ourselves, healing others: first in a series. Holist Nurs Pract. 2004;18:67-81.

science. Along with this, approximately fifty years ago, psychiatry began to change its focus to a biochemically based model of mental illness, and specific medications were developed by drug companies to treat these biochemical brain deficits. The brain became the latest mechanical part that once broken needed repair. Drug companies developed medications to treat deficiencies in the brain/mind to treat anxiety, depression, and other psychiatric diagnoses. While many of these developments and other scientific discoveries have helped patients, the changes also reinforced the reductionistic approach to healing as opposed to a more whole person approach, leaving body, mind, and spirit less integrated, not more integrated.

Eating disorders represent a spectrum of diagnoses in which this divide between body, mind, and spirit is particularly poignant. The hallmark of eating disorders is the inordinate and obsessive focus placed on one's superficial appearance. Sufferers exist in a narrow world in which their thoughts are consumed with self-judgment, criticism, fear, and anxiety about their appearance. The organic functions and sensations of the body are ignored to the point that people are able to ignore hunger cues or exercise to the point of grave injury without noticing the pain in their limbs. The body is a separate entity in the service of the disease, its function to live up to a dangerously unrealistic ideal.

Patients often feel stuck in a vortex of negative thinking best described by eating disorder patients themselves.

CASE EXAMPLE:

Arielle was diagnosed with BED. She had been overweight since childhood. In her mind, all of her problems were tied to her weight. If she could just lose weight, she would be better at her job, be happier, etc. When asked to depict how her thinking controlled her life in art, she drew a tornado made up of all the negative thoughts she constantly had: "I'm ugly. My thighs are big. I'm a pig. Nobody will ever love me. I hate myself." Emotions of shame, guilt, fear, and anger were also part of the tornado. Arielle felt she was being pulled down in her life by these negative thoughts and feelings and drew herself as being in the "eye of the tornado. I can't see any way to get out."

It was important for Arielle to begin to see her negative thinking as a separate part of herself, a life-size cardboard version of herself that she carried through life, her "ED-me." By making this distinction, she could begin to rebuild her true self from the small bits and pieces of memory she retained of her authentic, integral self. She remembered that she loved to wear dresses as a little girl, that pink was her favorite color, and that she loved to go to her grandmother's house and put on her grandma's lipstick. She remembered the feeling of playing dodgeball at school and how happy she'd been. She also could admit to herself that she was a good friend to others (although not to herself).

From these tiny threads, she began to weave a tapestry that didn't exclude the experience and acknowledgement of her eating disordered self. Rather, these threads would share space with an increasingly rich life quilt that she was re-creating.

The changes in medicine and science also affected the very core of medical education. In 1910, the Flexner report urged that financial support be given only to medical schools interested in using the new "scientific medicine" that promoted the use of prescription drugs and hospital-based technologies. The report found any discipline of medicine that did not use drugs to treat patients was equivalent to quackery and charlatanism. Prior to this time, homeopathic, chiropractic, and naturopathic medical schools were training medical practitioners alongside schools that taught what is now known as Western conventional medicine. This report had many excellent benefits, including the standardization of training for physicians. However, the conclusions were questioned because of the report's support from the American Medical Association, which predicted the demise of all osteopathic medical schools. The report was seen as being preferential to allopathic medicine. After this report, the majority of osteopathic, homeopathic, and chiropractic schools eventually closed and the shift toward what is now mainstream medical care was complete, thereby narrowing choices for patients and precluding the advancement of the new "scientific method" in the study of CAM therapies.[212]

In traditional systems of healing, patients are often able to recover parts of their soul or spirit that have been lost during their fierce struggle with their disease. Traditional medicine views the human body as a whole system in which mind, body, and spirit have equal value. This synergy as viewed from traditional Chinese medicine and is well described by Beinfield and Korngold in their book *Between Heaven and Earth: A Guide to Chinese Medicine.*[213]

Traditional systems view healing as an imbalance from which "dis-ease" occurs. The source of the imbalance could be internal (for example, emotional imbalances or unexpressed or "stuck" emotions) or external (such as environmental factors). These imbalances cause disruptions in the flow of vital energy through energy channels (sometimes called "meridians") in the body. Whenever there is a disruption of energy flow, there can be illness—mental, physical, or emotional. Healing requires restoration of the normal flow of energy.

Patients turn to CAM therapies because they provide immediate positive feedback. They offer an opportunity to deeply relax and there is an inherently pleasant feeling in just relaxing. CAM therapies also offer a reconnection of the mind to the "mind of our bodies,"[214] the intuitive sense that we all have but often ignore or have difficulty getting in touch with. This is what patients tap into when they do self-hypnosis and guided imagery as well as other types of mindful experiences. This is the part of us that knows beyond any doubt what our psychic and physical pain is all about. For example, when a patient says: "I feel anxious," this feeling of anxiety lives somewhere in the body. Many times, patients describe it as a ball or knot in the stomach, explaining the nausea that some experience in association with anxiety or fear. It may live in the chest and cause tightness and difficulty catching one's breath. Depression may "live" in the body as an empty space in the solar plexus, the energetic seat of our personal power. Not uncommonly, patients who have not felt as if they have a say in their lives or those whose feelings and wishes have not been validated as a young child describe pain in their heart or envision in imagery the insides of their heart being scarred and blackened, devoid of hope. In integrative medicine, metaphors for disease symptoms can serve as windows into the psyche allowing the practitioner to step into the patient's shoes and see through the patient's eyes.

If patients get in touch with the deeper meaning that the mind of our bodies knows about, it can be transformational. Tapping into that part of ourselves is like plugging into the main circuit board; the information delivered is not intellectual, but rather a felt sense of meaning on a deep level that resonates to the very core of our being. This is one reason why the combination of cognitive behavioral therapies (working in the mind) with CAM therapies (working with the "mind of our bodies" and with the body itself) pulls everything together and in an instant when all the "players" are sitting at the same "table," resolution of issues that have been in "mediation and discussion" for some time on the intellectual plane can be accomplished.

In Western culture there is an extreme emphasis on "looking a certain way"; there is little diversity in the accepted icons of beauty. This emphasis on such a narrow definition of beauty can contribute to the development of eating disorders and certainly is a trigger for relapse in those who are struggling to recover. Prescriptions for good health, including dietary ones, change from year to year and may vary widely one from another. One year, eating a high-carbohydrate diet is touted as the one and only diet to follow; at another time, we are told to limit carbs and focus on protein. There is no true ancestral wisdom in Western culture about eating, body size, or appearance. There is also no acceptance of individuality in appearance, what one eats, or how much one weighs. This has led to a sense that there is ONE right way to look: thin. One must be thin no matter what one's bone structure or genetic makeup. To be anything but thin is to be outside the norms of our culture and therefore, less accepted, less attractive, less worthy, less deserving of love. In the United States, concerns about weight and dissatisfaction with one's body are highly prevalent in third-grade children regardless of ethnicity or socio-economic status.[215] This trend shows the increasing preoccupation with appearance and being thin, beginning in early childhood. Traditional healing systems offer another way of looking at weight through the observations made thousands of years ago of naturally occurring body constitution and its associations with disease and behavior and health. These beliefs have stood the test of time and have changed very little despite changes in cultural mores about beauty.

There are many such traditional systems of healing. Ayurveda and traditional Chinese medicine are two that have been studied both in their countries of origin and by conventional medicine.

How does an understanding of or exposure to these traditional systems of healing inform the treatment of eating disorders? This information can provide a different lens through which to understand the beginnings of eating disorders as well as offer patients a more "universal" understanding of the root causes. Traditional systems of healing also offer tools to the practitioner for the treatment of eating disorders.

Ayurveda[*]

Over five thousand years ago, through what some consider divine inspiration, an elaborate system making up the "science of life" was handed down to a group of holy men, the *rishis*. This became the ancient Hindu text called the vedas. The vedic sciences are made up of four branches: self-knowledge, yoga, vedic astrology, and Ayurveda. Ayurveda focuses on health and healing and includes prescriptions for diet, use of herbs, and massage or body work. It is intended to support the body so that spiritual enlightenment can be obtained. Yoga can be roughly translated to mean "right path" and includes every aspect of life needed to be healthy and live in harmony with the world. Ayurvedic principles are used by 80 percent of the population in India and are used side by side with conventional or allopathic medicine.

The principles of Ayurveda emphasize the principle of "prana" or vital, primal energy, analogous to the TCM concept of "chi." Vital energy is taken in through the breath. Breath work is an integral component of mind-body medicine and can be useful in stress management and also is emphasized in Dialectical Behavior Therapy (DBT) mindfulness skills. Just as in TCM, there is an understanding that it is important for man to be aware of and connected to the environment. In Ayurveda, the five elements in nature (earth, air, fire, water, and ether) are thought to represent guidelines and principles from nature that are reflected in all aspects of our lives – health, illness, our individual constitutions and the way to maintain harmony. These elements derive from cosmic consciousness and manifest in matter on earth.[216]

[*] Note: discussion of complementary and alternative therapies is not meant to be exhaustive. Rather, a simplified version of these complex traditional systems of healing is presented with specific application to the treatment of eating disorders. References listed provide more detailed and complete information.

Aryuvedic principles also emphasize body constitution (doshas) as another manifestation of the elements on the individual level. The doshas determine our physiological and psychological makeup. Dietary prescriptions derive from one's *individual constitution,* not from popular culture or the media.

There are three doshas:

1. Vata (ether and air): Predominance of vata is found in people who tend toward being very active and, energetic and who like to always be in motion. They tend to fiddle a lot and may waste energy. In the same way, they may waste or fritter away their money. Often they prefer careers as artists or musicians and would rather not work for someone else.

2. Pitta (fire and water): Those with pitta constitutions tend to have fiery personalities with lots of anger, irritability, aggressiveness, and competitiveness. They tend to budget their money for the purpose of something useful.

3. Kapha (earth and water): People with Kapha predominance tend to be more solid with muscular strength, heavier, and slower moving. They may be also be more grounded and have a more stable personality. They tend to accumulate money.

An understanding of your constitution helps you to better understand the hand of cards you were dealt. You can understand your "habits and tendencies, such as being scatter-brained (vata), tendency to anger easily (pitta), or resistance to exercise (kapha) or physical problems such as overweight (kapha), ulcers (pitta) or constipation (vata)."[217] Understanding this whole-person philosophy toward body image, diet, and health opens up another way of looking at some of the problems our ED patients face. The importance in understanding an individualized approach to what we are supposed to look like, that each of us is born with an individual constitution or combination of doshas and that to be healthy, we must be true to our own nature, not to the expectations of the media or our peers or other *outside* influences, cannot be underestimated. It is a way of seeing in the intuitive sense that we must look *inside* ourselves for what is right for us, what is the best fit, and learning through this inside view to get back in touch with what our own bodies require for balance. Being more aware of health risks inherent in your inborn constitution may allow you to prevent some illnesses by adjusting your lifestyle to keep your doshas in balance.

This whole-person approach to health reminds us that we are integrally tied to nature—our own and the elements of nature in the environment. Our own nature includes our emotions and how we express them and acknowledges that if we repress emotions, this leads to imbalance. To remain in balance we must manage stress, avoid toxins, sleep well, and follow an eating program that keeps us in balance. These imbalances show up differently with different doshas or constitutions. For example, vata excess could describe many of the qualities seen in anorexics: anxious, negative thoughts, nervousness, and restless with bloating, poor digestion, cold in extremities, and exhaustion. Vatas and anorexics are often attracted to eating foods such as salads and uncooked vegetables when, under Ayurveda, they should eat sweet, sour, and salty tastes to balance their constitutions and warm, oily cooked foods to balance the cold, dry and light elements predominant in their constitution. It is not uncommon for anorexics to be vegetarians or even vegans; both diets are in opposition to the types of foods they should eat to restore their weight and return to a more balanced state. Vatas who are not in balance like to move and so are attracted to jogging or overexercising, which can cause them to be overtired. Vatas are also attracted to excessive sexual activity, which exacerbates vata imbalance. Think of comorbid diagnoses of sexual compulsivity, compulsive overexercise, and anxiety disorders—all not uncommon in the anorexic patient.

Ayurveda and eating disorders

One way to look at eating disorders from the Ayurvedic perspective is that the person substitutes a relationship with food for substantive relationships with others and to deal with the lack of congruence between himself and his place in the natural world or separateness from his or her own nature and from the natural cadence and synchronicity of life.

In parallel to anorexics, vatas may experience a great deal of fear, which is a symptom of imbalance. When in balance, they can be loving, creative, joyful, happy, and imaginative. When out of balance, they may experience fear of loneliness and other excessive fears; may be anxious and insecure; and may have difficulty thinking things through before acting, leading to poor judgment.

Pitta constitution people tend to be wise, intelligent, lovers of knowledge, problem solvers. Having things in order is important to them. Bulimics tend to exhibit the emotional and fiery nature of pitta predominance. When in balance, they are principled, which can lead to fanaticism. They can also be controlling and domineering. Factors that increase pitta are smoking cigarettes and eating too much spicy, fatty, or oily foods or sour and citrus fruits (such as grapefruits). Hot, humid weather can aggravate pitta constitutions, causing irritability and anger. Emotions of pitta excess include anger, hatred, and jealousy.

Kapha people have strong, healthy bodies. They tend to have slower metabolic rates; when out of balance, they will be overweight or obese. Simplistically, when imbalanced, kaphas are compulsive overeaters. They are usually attracted to sweet (watermelon, sweet fruit, cookies, cakes, dairy products), salty, and oily food. They should consume bitter, astringent, and pungent tastes. They may need coffee to get started in the morning and may feel lethargic after lunch. Kaphas often do not like to exercise, even though vigorous exercise is good for them. They often have sweet dispositions and are grounded and faithful people. But kapha excess can cause them to be greedy, lustful, possessive, lazy, and overly attached.

Chakras and childhood injury

Chakras are considered to be the centers of psychic energy and are located along the spinal cord. They are associated with the five elements of Ayurveda: earth, water, fire, air, and ether. Each chakra corresponds to developmental phases and specific developmental tasks. Each chakra is thought to have a specific sound and color. By meditating on these chakras, it is thought that people can gain mastery in their lives and over their bodies. Sometimes, an understanding of the chakra system can help those treating eating disorders to identify ages at which trauma—whether it is known or unknown—has occurred. Or, it may help with patients who are stuck in their emotional development. Chakra imbalances show up as developmental delays and as emotional or physical disorders.

Injuries or traumas to one chakra or another are what keep us from balance. Each chakra corresponds to an age range. If trauma or injury occurs at one of these ages, development can be delayed or injured.

DIAGRAM: Chakra locations [218]

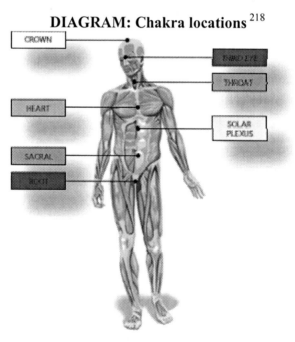

- 1st Chakra: Seat of Physical Body (ages 0-4)
  - Location: base of the spine
  - Physical conditions associated with imbalance: affects aging process, concerned with vitality, growth, and cell replacement.
  - Developmental stage: dependency on parents, asking lots of questions, "my feelings are more important than yours" (development of the ego); governs basic survival and sense of security, general health
  - Problems: weight gain, financial issues, constipation, fearfulness
  - Ways to open: yoga poses that strengthen feet and legs, i.e., lunges, breath work, resistance training

CASE EXAMPLE:

Jennifer, a twenty-year-old college student, suffered severe depression with chronic suicidality beginning when she left home to go to college. She had an enmeshed relationship with her mother and called her multiple times each day. She became a binge eater during college, gaining fifty pounds in her freshman year. She was easily frightened by any change in her support system, including having her therapist go on a short vacation. In treatment, Jennifer was taught self-soothing skills and breath work. Inner child work allowed her to strengthen her younger self and build up her adult ego state. Over time, she was able to begin the individuation process and to resume her college studies. She learned DBT skills to help her with emotional regulation.

- 2nd Chakra: Seat of Emotional Body (ages 0-7)
  - Location: just above the pubic bone.
  - Physical conditions: affects immune system

- o Developmental stage: compliant, sweet, helpful, attentive to others
- o Problems: addiction, emotional drama, workaholism, sexual problems, low back/hip pain
- o Ways to open: belly breathing

CASE EXAMPLE:

Rob, twenty-seven, was admitted for treatment of alcohol dependence and binge eating disorder. He reported being overweight since early childhood. He appeared and acted much younger than his chronological age and was overly involved with helping and being attentive to peers. He had difficulty in his relationships with women and didn't feel he was likeable. Rob's childhood was one of abuse alternating with neglect. His father in particular would rage at him, calling him "stupid" and saying he was "nothing." Rob had internalized his father's negative assessment and continued to retraumatize himself whenever he felt he had done something wrong. In treatment, he was able to begin healing work with his inner child, EMDR and Somatics for trauma and to address the adult insecurities he felt which originated in childhood.

- • 3rd Chakra: Seat of Mental Body (ages 0-12)
  - o Location: solar plexus; seat of personal power
  - o Physical conditions: affects digestive and endocrine system, eating disorders
  - o Developmental stage: ability to "digest" information, put in some order, awareness
  - o Problems: disempowerment, hatred, perfectionism
  - o Ways to open: following your passion, even in small things, doing things you truly enjoy (rather than what you should do)

Of note: modern causes of imbalance: excess television, video-games, lack of exercise, excess mental activity, nicotine, caffeine, alcohol, sugar

CASE EXAMPLE:

Janet presented for treatment with a history of bulimia since age fourteen. She was the oldest of three and the self-proclaimed "mediator" in her family. Her mother alternated between being kind and raging that "no one understands me." Her father was a workaholic. Janet identified with her mother and felt that she had to be "perfect so I don't cause more problems for my mother." Whenever her sisters wanted to argue about anything, Janet gave in so as not to cause problems. During her treatment, she struggled with always wanting to give her peers advice and with judging their behavior and with intellectualizing her problems. She had difficulty identifying anything she could do for fun or relaxation. With help, she was able to identify her family role and recognize the consequences of perfectionism. Over time, she began to individuate from her mother and to reconnect with her father.

- 4th Chakra: Seat of the Astral body. Heart Chakra (ages 0-18; colludes with the 3rd chakra to get rid of old or unnecessary thinking)
  - o Location: center of chest, heart
  - o Physical conditions: heart problems, lung and breast problems, and high blood pressure
  - o Developmental stage: development of tribal/group values; understanding of paradox
  - o Problems: shyness, lonely, isolated/withdrawn, jealousy, possessiveness
  - o Ways to open: exercises that open the chest, performing loving acts toward yourself and others, seeking support when lonely, self-care

CASE EXAMPLE:

Marjorie was thirty-four on admission for treatment of her long-standing anorexia (purge type). She presented as shy and withdrawn and had difficulty interacting with peers. She was reluctant to share in groups, especially about her current relationship with a woman who she described as "very codependent." With exploration, it became clear that Marjorie was extremely controlling and possessive in her relationship. She struggled in treatment with very concrete thinking and had trouble understanding concepts that conflicted with her "fantasy" viewpoint of herself and her life. Over time, she was able to begin to trust peers and staff and began slowly to share more of her story in groups. Marjorie was very ashamed to admit how insecure she felt, including feeling paranoid that others were talking about her or feelings of jealousy when peers didn't include her.

- 5th Chakra: Seat of Etheric body. (ages 0-25)
  o Location: throat
  o Physical conditions: thyroid problems, cervical neck tension, grinding teeth, hearing problems, excessive talking.
  o Developmental stage: development of one's voice, governed by the thyroid gland, the energy of which is about timing: speaking in or on time; nonverbal communication
  o Ways to open: quit smoking, singing, neck and shoulder exercises, expressing emotions, laughing out loud

CASE EXAMPLE:

Melanie admitted for treatment of night eating syndrome. Early in her admission, staff noticed that she had two distinct ways of speaking. One voice was very demure and soft; the other voice was loud and boisterous. Eventually, she explained that the quiet voice was the one she felt was more feminine and she avoided using the "loud" voice that came more naturally.

She even had a name for the "loud" voice. She called it "Martin." It became apparent in treatment that she had not felt her "true voice" was supported growing up. Often, people complimented her when she spoke in the softer voice, which made her seem less threatening. Melanie was able to admit to feeling fearful of alienating people with her true voice. In treatment, she received feedback that supported her true voice and encouragement to allow her true self to "shine."

- 6th Chakra: Seat of Celestial body (ages 0-50)
  o Location: center of lower forehead just above eyebrows
  o Physical conditions: headaches, poor memory, sinus, hearing, ADHD, autism
  o Developmental stage: middle age/practical wisdom, able to understand more profound information, development of intuition, imagination
  o Emotional: feeling stuck in old thought patterns,
  o Ways to open: use positive affirmations, finding opportunities to experience awe/inspiration

CASE EXAMPLE:

Tamara, forty-nine, had a lifelong history of compulsive overeating and a two-year history of alcohol dependence. The patient suffered a back injury as a result of a motor vehicle accident and had chronic pain that made it difficult for her to work. She eventually went on disability. She complained of chronic headaches since the accident and had hearing loss in the right ear. Tamara was admitted for pain management and treatment of her ED. During her treatment, she began to identify old patterns of not speaking up for herself and of caretaking others at her own expense, creating strain and emotional pain. She received massage, chiropractic, and acupuncture for treatment of her pain and was weaned off oxycodone. As her pain lessened, Tamara began to get back in touch with her passion for drawing and journaling and her love of nature. In meditation class, she was able to reconnect with her spirituality, which was a source of strength and comfort to her.

- 7th Chakra: seat of the Ketheric body. (ageless)
  o Location: the very top of the skull
  o Physical conditions: brain diseases, Alzheimer's
  o Developmental stage: governs issues about life or death, superconsciousness, control issues, connection with the divine.
  o Problems: greed, profound detachment, feelings of superiority
  o Ways to open: meditation[219]

CASE EXAMPLE:

Joseph, forty-nine, was admitted for treatment of binge eating disorder with recent episodes of purging of which he was quite ashamed. He worked as a classical musician, but reported "I've lost all interest in my music since my daughter died." The daughter had been killed in a car accident less than one year before at age twenty-two. After her death, he and his wife began to fight and eventually separated. Joseph appeared older than his stated age and presented with anger alternating with sadness. He reported having no spiritual connection and despite having other grown children, said "I just don't know if I can go on." During treatment, Joseph worked on his grief and loss issues and on his anger at God for "taking my precious daughter." He had zero balancing and for the first time in his treatment was able to cry. In guided imagery, he reported having an "epiphany." "I began to feel my daughter's presence and felt as if I could talk to her as if she was right here. I told her that I loved her and apologized for not being closer to her when she was younger (due to his travel for work). I felt as if she forgave me and that was a big load off my chest." In meditation, Joseph reported feeling a "sense of God taking over my job as my daughter's father. I could release her to God for safekeeping."

The cases above provide an alternative way of seeing eating disorders and even though the concepts may be unfamiliar, can often mirror what we observe clinically. They all have in common a whole-person approach to healing. Healing methods originate from the understanding and belief in the body as an energetic organism with the power to heal itself. Traditional Chinese medicine also offers another lens through which to view the transformational potential of this profound understanding of the self-healing nature of the human organism.

Traditional Chinese Medicine (TCM)

The principles of TCM date back to over three thousand years and were first described in detail in *The Yellow Emperor's Classic of Internal Medicine* during the Han dynasty. Treatments included in TCM include acupuncture, the use of Chinese herbs, manipulative therapy, food cures, and therapeutic exercises— qi gong and tai chi. In China, physicians in medical school can choose to specialize in either conventional Western medicine or TCM, which are practiced side by side. TCM can treat many illnesses that don't respond to conventional medical treatments. TCM physicians use pulse diagnosis; examination of the complexion and the tongue; and listening to a patient's symptoms, food preferences, and eating patterns. TCM focuses on causes of disease, not just symptoms, and is useful in treating skin disorders, some chronic diseases, and pain syndromes.

One of the keys to understanding TCM is the philosophy of yin and yang. In simple terms, yin is the feminine principle and yang the male principle. Health is considered to be related to the interplay between yin and yang. In parallel to the Ayurvedic medicine concept of prana is the concept of chi or qi also known as one's vital life force.

The causes of illness under TCM include external factors such as wind, summer heat, dampness, dryness, fire, and cold; the seven emotions of joy, anger, worry, contemplation, sorrow, fear, and shock; foods; and fatigue. When foods are the cause of disease, it is related to overeating, intoxication, and eating foods that exacerbate imbalances in yin or yang or prolonged consumption of greasy foods. Fatigue can be due to excessive sexual activity or be due to deficiencies in various organ systems.

Food cures are a particularly interesting part of TCM treatments. Food is seen as a therapeutic tool, used to treat diseases and symptoms. While the Western diet looks at food content of protein, fat, carbohydrates, and calories, the Chinese diet considers food for their energies, movements, flavors, and actions. Similar to Ayurvedic diet prescriptions, TCM diet flavors include pungent, sweet, sour, bitter, and salty with each having a different effect on the body. Some foods have only one flavor; others may have multiple flavors.

Treatments in Chinese medicine include the use of herbs, acupuncture, moxibustion, Shiatsu, Chinese massage, and qi gong. Herbs are used to balance disharmony in the body. Acupuncture involves the insertion of tiny, sterile needles at various points on the energy channels or meridians of the body. Other treatments in TCM include moxibustion (the burning of moxa, an herb, at an acupuncture point); massage or Shiatsu (acupressure); and the use of qi gong (originating from martial arts and involving meditation, relaxation, and visualization).

Acupuncture has been studied both in the West and in China and has been shown to activate the body's electrical system, the blood, and nervous systems and to result in the release of endorphins and other neurotransmitters that inhibit pain. The American Foundation of Medical Acupuncture in a review of the world clinical literature showed efficacy of acupuncture in the treatment of pain, substance abuse, gynecological problems, depression, and anxiety. There was also efficacy shown for cardiovascular, respiratory, gastrointestinal, skin, urological, and neurological problems.[220]

TCM, eating disorders and comorbid conditions:

Most studies on the benefits of TCM have been done in China. There are no studies in English specifically addressing the use of acupuncture to treat eating disorders. Studies on the use of acupuncture for obesity have postulated that the mechanism for any benefit derives from acupuncture's effect on appetite, intestinal motility, metabolism, and stress reaction, including the release of beta endorphins and serotonin.

Other studies on acupuncture relate to the treatment of comorbid conditions of depression and substance use disorder. A Cochrane database review found no evidence that medication was better than acupuncture in reducing the severity of mild to moderate depression. Poor study design and small numbers limited the strength of the conclusion.[221] A review of seven randomized comparative trials suggested that electroacupuncture is as effective as antidepressant medication.[222] A study of acupuncture for major depression in women produced equivalent results to other validated treatments.[223]

Many anecdotal reports show reduction in drug withdrawal symptoms with acupuncture. In one study of cocaine/crack abusers, acupuncture was compared with placebo acupuncture; both groups reported a significant reduction in drug usage.[224] Auricular (ear) acupuncture was not found to be more effective in treating cocaine abuse compared with either sham acupuncture or conventional treatment without acupuncture.[225]

Eating disorders from the perspective of Five Element Acupuncture:

The five elements in TCM refer to the interrelationship between water, earth, wood, fire, and metal. Through observation of patients treated at an inpatient facility for drug, alcohol, eating disorders, and mood disorders (Sierra Tucson in Tucson, Arizona), a correlation between the five elements and disease diagnosis was seen as:

- Wood: alcohol, cocaine, anger issues
- Water: depression and trauma
- Metal: anorexia
- Earth: codependency
- Fire: mood disorders[226]

For example, when metal constitution is out of balance, the physical pathology includes asthma and other lung problems, ulcerative colitis, diarrhea and constipation, eczema and all skin disorders, poor endurance, and fatigue. The psychological pathology includes perfectionism, withdrawal and isolation, loneliness or needing companionship, cruelty, wanting revenge, filled with regrets, rigidity, grief, and depression.

CASE EXAMPLE: More on Tara

When referred to the five-element acupuncturist, Tara was told she had metal constitution. At first, she expressed frustration at being given "one more label. Now, I'm anorexic, drug addict, trauma survivor, and metal constitution." The meaning and signs of imbalance were discussed with her, and she was asked to reflect on this and see what fit. When she was next seen, she came in very excited and said: "I can't believe it but I can see that my metal is out of balance everywhere in my life. My house has metal everywhere. My kitchen has stainless steel appliances and metal countertops. My furniture is very metallic. Everywhere around me, there are cold, rigid surfaces and not one little bit of anything soft or warm." Tara began to see how metal constitution imbalances in her body were being reflected in her life. By using symptoms of imbalance of metal, she was able to have another tool for monitoring her progress in recovery. For example, her perfectionism when in balance was a good skill in her business ventures; when out of balance, it looked more like obsessive-compulsive disorder. Her anxiety when in balance was what made her a "high energy" person. Over time, with proper nutrition and a more balanced approach to exercise and ongoing acupuncture treatment, her skin rash faded. Acupuncture may have also been helpful in the return of her menstrual cycle after more than one year. Tara reported decreases in her anxiety during and immediately after receiving her acupuncture treatments as well.[227]

Summary

Our current Western approach to body size is influenced by culture and whatever the prevailing research dictates about a healthy diet. This information changes frequently and causes confusion amongst those who are overweight and want to lose weight or those of normal weight who feel they should be thinner. This explains in part the increase in eating disorders over the last fifty years. In the 1950s, popular icons of beauty were of normal weight with a curvy, feminine physique. More recent icons are painfully thin with bodies altered by plastic surgery to fit the current ideal.

These ancient traditions are just that—ancient. They have not changed over thousands of years and are part of a whole-person approach to eating for good health. Eating for health involves an individualized understanding of body types, energy balance, and foods that fit our constitutions. An example of how this is validated in modern experience can be seen in the cravings that our bodies feel whenever we go on restricted diets. Some people will crave carbohydrates when on the high-protein, high-fat diets; fasting diets often lead to craving crunchy foods. The ancient Ayurvedic traditions prescribe a variety of flavors (pungent, salty, sweet, etc.) to be eaten at each meal. They suggest certain foods be avoided in certain illnesses and prescribe the use of other foods for healing disease.

They also offer another way of seeing body weight—through an ancient system focused on an individualized approach to healing of body, mind, and spirit through right eating, activity, and spiritual practice. Rather than defining "good foods" versus "bad foods" or focusing on fat, protein, and carbohydrate grams or calories, these traditional methods are part of a whole system of healing and seek to restore balance to the individual through nutrition. Western nutrition examines body weight and body mass index. Traditional medicine looks at body constitution or psychobiological function whose definitions derive from observation of the huge variety of differences and preferences of the individual when in a balanced state or when out of balance. The doshas, for example, are like our individual fingerprints; they identify characteristics not of weight or body size but of nutritional needs that correlate with psychological and cognitive functioning. Therefore, this way of seeing our physical bodies does not promote dieting or identify ANY ideals other than the ideal of each individual finding his or her own particular balanced state of being. In this scenario, nutrition is one of the keys to well-being and good health.

In conclusion, understanding the philosophy behind complementary alternative systems of healing enables practitioners to see and address eating disorders through the lens of traditional medicine's emphasis on balance in the entire individual system and by reuniting and healing body, mind, and spirit.

CHAPTER 11
ARE WE THERE (IN RECOVERY) YET?

Illness is a call to action. The call will get louder and more urgent if not answered. If you choose to answer the call, you will be taking the first step on your journey to healing.
Carolyn Ross, MD *Miracles in Healing*

Recovery is the journey of a lifetime, one that requires the ability to embrace chaos rather than control, to live in a series of questions, the ability to recognize that life in recovery is like being on a seesaw (teeter-totter). What is the difference between embracing chaos and creating chaos, which is what being in the disease does? Creating chaos is the coping mechanism often developed in response to life circumstances that are either traumatic or too overwhelming. Persons who create chaos may be labeled as having borderline personality disorder. In this sense, chaos conforms to our felt sense about chaos, in which life feels and appears to be completely without order. In mathematical chaos theory, systems are orderly in some sense and deterministic. For example, weather is a chaotic system whose statistics (climate) are not chaotic. From this point of view, chaotic systems have specific characteristics:

- *A small change in the current pattern of behavior can lead to markedly different future behavior.* An example of this is the popularly known "butterfly effect," the theory that when a butterfly flaps its wings over Tokyo, it creates tiny atmospheric changes that over time cause a tornado in Texas. In recovery, moment-to-moment decisions and actions can support or destroy a recovery program. Choosing not to walk down a certain street, to call one's sponsor, or to go to a meeting are all small changes that can affect future behavior.

- *The system will evolve over time so that different aspects will overlap with other regions like the mixing of colored dyes.* Early recovery often looks like a patchwork quilt, with each patch a different insight or lesson learned. The red patch may symbolize learning that anger at your father can be linked to dysfunctional relationships with other men; the purple patch, an insight that feeling trapped in childhood with a mother who is mentally ill can be played out in one's choice of career and marriage; the paisley patch, understanding that core beliefs such as "big is better" or "showing your feelings is a sign of weakness" have dramatically affected your life; and so on. If recovery continues over time, what needs to happen would be akin to what would happen to the patchwork quilt if the colors ran together so each square contains parts of the colors of the whole quilt. There must be integration of insight, behavior, and emotion into the body-mind-spirit system for true transformative recovery.

Chaos theory became popular after the middle of the twentieth century when scientists found that linear theory, the prevailing theory of how systems work, could not explain observed phenomenon in the environment.

How is this relevant to recovery? Most people entering into recovery want to have more control over their lives, perhaps feeling that control is the answer to the puzzle of chaos that they created in their disease. *What you resist persists.* Their concept of recovery can be flawed to begin with. The black-and-white thinking common in eating disorder patients does not stop entirely when recovery begins. In this way of thinking, life is either chaotic or peaceful, one is either happy or sad, either madly in love or convinced that one's partner is no good. One way of "doing" recovery from eating disorders is to "follow the rules," but to do so in the same way as the eating disorder was done. How does this look? Well, the anorexic who no longer restricts will follow a rigid meal plan without deviation, avoiding foods that are different or uncomfortable. Relationships may be avoided entirely to prevent risking failure if the relationship does not turn out to be perfect.

In successful recovery, it is necessary to find and **live in the grays of life**, between failure and success, to learn to work and live in the middle ground apart from the highs and lows and extremes that define the disease. Of course, this process takes time and hard work. What may have looked like anxiety and obsessive-compulsive behaviors in the disease can, when in balance, allow a person to be good in a business that requires attention to detail.

Just as in mathematics, recovery is not linear. You can't always predict what will happen next; that is what makes recovery such a dangerous opportunity. If you don't practice recovery enough, you can become stuck in your insights and your understanding of the experiences that led to insights will harden into something solid that can't be changed. Then your recovery becomes, as it does for many, a memory of an experience rather than the experience itself. You will go through life trying to live up to this fixed, engraved in stone concept that you call "recovery" but that may or may not apply to what is happening in your life currently.

The bigger the insights or epiphanies, the more likely they are to become a concept on which you can hang your hat. They become the sound bites of your recovery process rather than just one of many steps along the journey to recovery. This is dangerous because life is constantly changing and evolving. The insights you had as a twenty-year-old drug addict, other than the quintessential concept of the need to stop using drugs, may become fixed in such a way that they impede your growth and development when you are forty or fifty.

CASE EXAMPLE:

Michael, went through treatment for cocaine addiction at the age of thirty and stayed sober for many years. During those years, however, he developed a cross-addiction to sex and engaged in orgies, went to sex clubs, and had multiple partners. This seemed acceptable to him until he realized at forty that he had no permanent relationships. In an attempt to change his life, he began to stop having sex with multiple partners, but to do so, he used food to quell his insecurities and to suppress his emotions of shame and loneliness, and his fear of growing old alone. He entered treatment for binge eating disorder and presented as very unemotional. He had difficulty even identifying any core feelings during his group processes. During treatment, however, he began to get back in touch with the same emotions that initially fueled the need to numb his feelings with drugs. While he had no desire to return to using cocaine, he had developed several cross-addictions that served the same purpose of distracting him from his feelings and from issues in his life. The insights he had gained at thirty had more to do with his feelings of insecurity due to issues from his childhood. At forty, he began to see these insights as just one piece of the complex puzzle of his life. He began to look at his career choices, to acknowledge a history of sexual molestation at the age of twelve he had never told anyone about, to learn more about his issues with women, and so on. Had he not crystallized his recovery as belonging to just the issue of using drugs, he might have used that initial issue as a springboard for deeper exploration. In this scenario of recovery, family visits during the holidays would have been acknowledged as being very triggering for him, forcing him to examine his relationship with his siblings and his role in the family. His issues with women could have been detected in his multiple partners and the lack of any sustained relationships.

Recovery can take shape in many different ways. One must be willing to, in the end, do whatever it takes to move down the cascade of behaviors, emotions, bodily sensations, and core beliefs in the discovery of one's nature and passion. Then, the flow should reverse and one's passion should determine behaviors, beliefs, emotions, and bodily sensations.

There are many different ways to find healing from eating disorders. The integrative medicine approach offers many options to explore and experience. While research into these therapies is in the early stages, overall, they offer therapies that provide immediate benefit with very little risk. Their focus on addressing the needs of the whole person offer the potential for true transformation.

Eating disorders and their comorbid diagnoses, like other illnesses, are a call to action. The call should alert one to the disharmony that exists between oneself and one's nature or one's authetic self. To answer the call is to embark on a journey whose only destination is the restoration and continued equilibration of balance. This journey should not end when the siren call is less insistent, but rather become part of the fabric of a life well lived in the search of wellness of body, mind, and spirit.

[1] Unutzer J, Klap R, Sturm R, et al. Mental disorders and the use of alternative medicine: results from a national survey. Am J Psychiatry. 2000 Nov;157(11):1851-7.

[2] Knaudt PR, Connor KM, Weisler RH, et al. Alternative therapies use by psychiatric outpatients. J Nerv Ment Dis. 1999 Nov;187(11):692-5..

[3] Kessler RC, Soukup J, Davis RB, et al. The use of complementary and alternative therapies to treat anxiety and depression in the United States. Am J Psychiatry. 2001 Feb;158(2):289-94.

[4] Eisenberg DM, Davis RB, Ettner SL, et al. Trends in alternative medicine use in the United States, 1990-1997: results of a follow-up national survey. JAMA. 1998 nov 11;280(18):1569-75.

[5] Altman, D. Meal by Meal. Makawao, HI: Inner Ocean Publishing, 2004.

[6] Shaw H,et al. Body image and eating disturbances across ethnic groups: More similarities than differences. Psych of Addic Behav, 18(1):12-18.

[7] Cachelin FM et al. (2003) Dieting and its relationship to smoking, acculturation, and family environment in Asian and Hispanic adolescents. Eating Disorders, 11:51-61.

[8] Sanchez-Johnson L et al. (2003) Binge eating and eating-related cognitions and behavior in ethnically diverse obese women. Obesity Research, 11:1002-9.

[9] O'Neill SK (2003) African American women and eating disturbances: A meta-analysis. Journal of Black Psychology, 29(1):3-16.

[10] Lynch WC et al. (2004) Eating attitudes of Native American and White female adolescents: a comparison of BMI-and age-matched groups. Ethnicity & Health, 9(3):253-66.

[11] Halmi KA. The multimodal treatment of eating disorders. World Psychiatry. 2005 June;4(2):69-73

[12] Keel PK, Dorer DJ, Eddy KT, et al. Predictors of mortality in eating disorders. Arch Gen Psychiatry. 2003 Feb;60(2):179-83.

[13] Stice E, Burton EM, Shaw H. Prospective relations between bulimic pathology, depression, and substance abuse: unpacking comorbidity in adolescent girls.

[14] Sullivan PF. Mortality in anorexia nervosa.Am J Psychiatry 1995 Jul;152 (7), 1073-1074

[15] Franko DL, Keel PK, Dorer DJ, et al. What predicts suicide attempts in women with eating disorders? Psychol Med. 2004 Jul;34(5):843-53.

[16] Brumberg JJ: Fasting girls: The emergence of anorexia nervosa as a modern disease. Cambridge, Mass. Harvard University Press. 1988

[17] Miller MN, Pumariega AJ. Culture and eating disorders: a historical and cross-cultural review. Psychiatry. 2001 Summer;64(2):93-110.

[18] The Eating Disorders Sourcebook: A comprehensive guide to the causes, treatment and prevention of eating disorders. (2nd Edition). 1999. Lowell House, Lincolnwood, Illinois.

[19] Minuchin S, Rosman BL, Baker L. Psychosomatic Families: Anorexia nervosa in Context. Cambridge Mass. Harvard University Press: 1978.

[20] Rusca R. An existentialist approach to anorexia nervosa. Am J Psychother.2003;57(4): 491-498.

[21] Wilson GT & Shafran R. Eating disorders guidelines from NICE. The Lancet, 2005; 365:79-81.

[22] Psychiatric Services. APA Publishes revised practice guideline for treating eating disorders. Jan 2000, 51:1.

[23] Wonderlich S, Mitchell JE, de Zwaan M, Steiger H (editors). Annual Review of Eating Disorders, Part 2-2006. Oxford, England, Radcliffe Publishing.

[24] Hay P, Bacaltchuk J, Claudino A, et al. Individual psychotherapy in the outpatient treatment of adults with anorexia nervosa. The Cochrane Library, issue 3. John Wiley & Sons, Ltd. Chichester, UK (www.thecochranelibrary.com)

[25] The Cochrane Database of Systematic Reviews 2006 Issue 4 Copyright © 2006 The Cochrane Collaboration. Published by John Wiley and Sons, Ltd.

[26] Fichter MM, Quadflieg N, Gnutzmann A. Binge Eating Disorder: treatment outcome over a 6-year course. J Psychosom Res. 1998 Mar-Apr;44(3-4):385-405.

[27] Colquitt J, Clegg A, Loveman E, Royle P, Sidhu MK. Surgery for morbid obesity. *Cochrane Database of Systematic Reviews* 2005, Issue 4. Art. No.: CD003641. DOI: 10.1002/14651858.CD003641.pub2.

[28] The Cochrane Database of Systematic Reviews 2006 Issue 4, Copyright © 2006 The Cochrane Collaboration. Published by John Wiley and Sons, Ltd.

[29] Taylor HL, Keys A. Adaptation to Caloric Restriction. Science, New Series. 1950 Aug 25; 112(2904):215-218.

[30] Kalm LM, Semba RD. They Starved So That Others Could Be Better Fed: Remembering Ancel Keys and the Minnesota Experiment 2005 The American Society for Nutritional Sciences J. Nutr. 135:1347-1352, June 2005.

[31] Latner JD, Wilson GT. Binge eating and satiety in bulimia nervosa and binge eating disorder: Effects of macronutrient intake. Int J of Eating Disorders, 2004; 36:402-15.

[32] Dalvit-McPhillips S. A dietary approach to bulimia treatment. Physiol Behav. 1984 Nov; 33(5):769-75.

[33] Cass H and Holford P. Natural Highs: Feel Good all the Time. Avery, a member of Penguin Group USA. 2002, page 157-8.

[34] Coppen A, Bolander-Gouaille C. Treatment of depression: time to consider folic acid and vitamin B12. J Psychopharmacol. 2005 Jan; 19(1):59-65.

[35] Taylor MJ, Carney S, Geddes J, Goodwin G. Cochrane Review. "Folate for depressive disorders" The Cochrane Library, Issue 2, 2006. Chichester, UK: John Wilen & Sons, Ltd.

[36] "Folic Acid" Alternative Medicine Review, Vol 10 (3). 2005: 222-229.

[37] Lake, J. The Integrative Management of Depressed Mood. Integrative Medicine 2004 June/July; 3(1):48-57.

[38] Cass H, Holford P. Natural Highs: Feel Good all the Time. Avery (a member of Penguin Group (USA)2002, New York, NY.

[39] Bilici M, et al. Double-blind, placebo-controlled study of zinc sulfate in the treatment of attention deficit hyperactivity disorder. Prog. Neuropsypharmacol Biol Psychiatry. 2004 Jan;28(1):181-90

[40] Katz RL, et al. Zinc deficiency in anorexia nervosa. J Adolesc Health Care. 1987 Sep;8(5):400-6.

[41] Birmingham CL, Goldner EM, Bakan R. Controlled trial of zinc supplementation in anorexia nervosa. Int J Eat Disord. 1994 Apr;15(3):251-5.

[42] Ebbesson So, et al. Omega-3 fatty acids improve glucose tolerance and components of the metabolic syndrome in Alaskan Eskimos: the Alaska Siberia project. Int J Circumpolar Health. 2005 Sep;64(4):396-408.

[43] Harris WS. N-3 fatty acids and serum lipoproteins: human studies. Am J Clin Nutr 1997;65:1645S-54S.

[44] Covington MB. Omega-3 Fatty Acids. American Family Physician, 2004 July 1. Vol. 70(1):133-40

[45] Peet M, Horrobin DF. A dose-ranging study of the effects of ethyl-eicosapentanoate in patients with ongoing depression despite apparently adequate treatment with standard drugs. Arch Gen Psychiatry. 2002 Oct;59(10):913-9.

[46] Nemets B, et al. Addition of omega-3 fatty acid to maintenance medication treatment for recurrent unipolar depressive disorder. Am J Psychiatry. 2002 Mar; 159(3):477-9.

[47] Stoll AL, Severus WE, Freeman MP, et al. Omega 3 fatty acids in bipolar disorder: a preliminary double-blind, placebo-controlled trial. Arch Gen Psychiatry, 1999 May;56(5):407-12.

[48] Zanarini MC, Frankenburt FR. Omega-3 Fatty Acid treatment of women with borderline personality disorder: a double-blind, placebo-controlled pilot study. Am J Psychiatry. 2003 Jan;160(1):167-9.

[49] Fontani G, et al. Cognitive and physiological effects of Omega-3 polyunsaturated fatty acid supplementation in healthy subjects. Eur J Clin Invest. 2005 Nov;35(11):691-9.

[50] Matkovic V, Goel PK, Badenhop-Stevens NE, et al. Calcium supplementation and bone mineral density in females from childhood to young adulthood: a randomized controlled trial. Am J Clin Nutr. 2005;81:168-74.

[51] Dodiuk-Gad RP, Rozen GS, Rennert G, et al. Sustained effect of short-term calcium supplementation on bone mass in adolescent girls with low calcium intake. Am J Clin Nutr. 2005;81:168-74.

[52] Bonjour J-P, Chevalley T, Ammann P, et al. Gain in bone mineral mass in pre-pubertal girls 3.5 years after discontinuation of calcium supplementation: a follow-up study. Lancet. 2001;358:1208-1212.

[53] Gibbons MJ, Gilchrist NL, Frampton C, et al. The effects of a high calcium dairy food on bone health in pre-pubertal children in New Zealand. Asia Pac J Clin Nutr. 2004;13:341-347.

[54] Courteix D, Jaffre C, Lespessailles E, Benhamou L. cumulative effects of calcium supplementation an dphysical activity on bone accretion in premenarchal children: a double-blind randomized placebo-controlled trial. Int J Sports Med. 2005;25(5):332-8

[55] Dawson-Hughes B. Calcium and vitamin D for bone health in adults. In: Holick MF, Dawson-Hughes B, eds. Nutrition and Bone Health. Holick Totowa, NJ: Humana Press; 2004:197-210. (as seen "Nutritional Influences on Bone Health: An Update on Current Research and clinical Implications by susan Lanham-New. www.medscape.com

[56] Shea B, Wells G, Cranney A, et al; Osteolporosis Methodology Group; Osteoporosis Researdch Advisory Group. Calcium supplementation on bone loss in postmenopausal women. Cochrane Database Syst Rev. 2004;(1):CD004526.

[57] Van der Mei IA, Ponsonby AI, Dwyer T, et al. Past exposure to sun, skin phenotype and risk of multiple sclerosis: case-dontrol study. BMJ 2003:327:316.

[58] Van der Mei IA, Ponsonby AI, Blizzard L, Dwyer T. Regional variation in multiple sclrosis prevalence in Australia and its association with ambient ultraviolet radiation. Neuroepidemiology 2001;20:168-74.

[59] Kurtzke JF. A reassessment of the distribution of multiple sclerosis. Part one. Acta Neurol Scand. 1975; 51:110-136.

[60] Kurtzke JF, Beebe GW, Norman JE JR. Epidemiology of multiple sclerosis in U.S. veterans: 1. Race, sex and geographic distribution. Neurology 1979;29:1228-35.

[61] Wallin MT, Page WF, Kurtzke JF. Multiple sclerosis in US veterans of the Vietnam era and later military service: race, sex and geography. Ann Neurol 2004;55:65-71.

[62] Luscombe CJ, Fryer AA, French ME, et al. Exposure to ultraviolet radiation: association with susceptibility and age at presentation with prostate cancer. Lancet 2001; 358:641-2.

[63] Smedby KE, Hjalgrim H, MElbye M, et al. Ultraviolet radiation exposure and risk of malignant lymphomas. J Natl Cancer Inst 2005;97: 199-209. All above from Alternative Medicine Review Vol 10, no. 2, 2005

[64] Plotnikoff GA, Quigley JM. Prevalence of severe hypovitaminosis D in patients with persistent, nonspecific musculoskeletal pain. Mayo Clin Proc. 2003;78:1463-70.

[65] Plotnikoff GA, Quigley JM. Prevalence of severe hypovitaminosis D in patients with persistent, nonspecific musculoskeletal pain. Mayo Clinic Proc. 2003 Dec;78(12):1463-70.

[66] Gordon CM, Nelson LM. Amenorrhea and bone health in adolescents and young women. Curr Opin Obstet Gynecol. 2003 Oct;15(5):377-384.

[67] Meyer HE, Smedshaug GB, Kvaavik E, et al. Can vitamin D supplementation reduce the risk of fracture in the elderly? A randomized controlled trial. J Bone Miner Res. 2002;17:709-15.

[68] Bonjour JP. Dietary protein: an essential nutrient for bone health. J Am Coll Nutr.2005;24(6Suppl):526S-536S.

[69] Appel LJ, Moore TJ, Obarzanek E, et al. A clinical trial of the effects of dietary patterns on blood pressure. N Engl J Med. 1997;336:1117-24.

[70] Lin P, Ginty F, Appel L, et al. The DASH diet and sodium reduction improve markers of bone turnover and calcium metabolism in adults. J Nutr. 2001;133:3130-6.

[71] Tylvasky FA, Holliday K, Danish R, et al. Fruit and vegetable intakes are an independent predictor of bone size in early pubertal children. Am J Clin Nutr. 2004;79:311-17.

[72] Armas LAG, Hollis BW and Heaney RP. Vitamin D2 is much less effective than vitamin D3 in Humans. The J of Clinical Endocrinology and Metabolism; 89(11):5387-91.

[73] Konstantynowicz J, Kadziela-Olech H, Kaczmarski M, et al. J Clin Endocrinol MEtab. 2005 Sep;90(9):5382-5. Epub 2005 Jun 7.

[74] Miller KK. Mechanisms by which nutritional disorders cause reduced bone mass in adults. J Womens Health (Larchmt). 2003 Mar:12(2):145-50.

[75] Heer M, Mika C, Grzella I, et al. Changes in bone turnover in patients with anorexia nervosa during eleven weeks of inpatient dietary treatment. Clin Chem, 2002 May;48(5):754-60.

[76] Sanders ME. Considerations for use of probiotic bacteria to modulate human health. J Nutr 2000;130:384S-390S.

[77] Wollowski I, Rechkemmer G, Pool-Zobel BL. Protective role of probiotics and prebiotics in colon cancer. Am J Clin Nutr. 2001;73:451S-455S.

[78] Brady LJ, Gallaher DD, Busta FF. The role of probiotic cultures in the prevention of colon cancer. J Nutr. 2000;130:410S-414S.

[79] Khalif IL, Quigley EM, Konovitch EA, Maximova ID. Alterations in the colonic flora and intestinal permeability and evidence of immune activation in chronic constipation. Dig Liver Dis. 2005 Nov;37(11):838-49.

[80] Kajander K, Hatakka K, Poussa T, A probiotic mixture alleviates symptoms in irritable bowel syndrome patients: a controlled 6-month intervention. Aliment Pharmacol Ther. 2005 Sep 1;22(5):387-94.

[81] Koebnick C, Wagner I, Leitzmann P, et al. Probiotic beverage containing Lactobacillus casei Shirota improves gastrointestinal symptoms in patients with chronic constipation. Can J Gastroenterol. 2003 Nov;17(11):655-9.

[82] Kohnen R, Oswald WD. The effects of valerian, propranolol and their combination on activation, performance, and mood of healthy volunteers under social stress conditions. Pharmacopsychiatry 1988;21:447-8 (as seen in Alt Med Review vol 9 no. 4 2004.

[83] Andreatini R, Sartori VA, Seabra ML, Leite JR. Effect of valepotriates (valerian extract) in generalized anxiety disorder: a randomized placebo-controlled pilot study. Phytother Res 2002; 16:650-4.

[84] Cropley M, Cave Z, Ellis J, Middleton RW. Effect of kava and valerian on human physiological and psychological responses to mental stress assessed under laboratory conditions. Phytother Res 2002;16:23-7

[85] Ara DerMarderosian, Lawrence Liberti, John A Beutler, and Constance Grauds. Review of natural products, 1999 ed. From Facts and Comparisons, St. Louis Mo.

[86] Schmidt-Vogt J. Treatment of nervous sleep disturbances and inner restlessness with a purely herbal sedative. Therapiewoche 1986;36:663-7.

[87] Leathwood PD, Chauffard F, Heck E, Munoz-Box R. Aqueous extract of valerian root improves sleep quality in man. Pharmacol Biochem Behav 1982;17:65-71.

[88] Trevena L. Sleepless in Sydney – is valerian an effective alternative to benzodiazepines in treatment of insomnia? ACP J Club. 2004;141:A14-16.

[89] Ziegler G, Ploch M, Miettinem-Baumann A, et al. Efficacy and tolerability of valerian extract L1 156 compared with oxazepam in the treatment of non-organic insomnia-a randomized, double-blind, comparative clinical study. Eur J Med Res 2002;7:480-6.

[90] Poyares DR, Guilleminault C, Ohayon MM, Tufik S. Can valerian improve the sleep of insomniacs after benzodiazepine withdrawal? Prog Neurpsychophamaracol Biol Psychiatry 2002;26:539-45.

[91] Morin CM, Koetter U, Bastien C, et al. Valerian-hops combination and diphenhydramine for treating insomnia: a randomized placebo-controlled clinical trial. Sleep. 2005 Nov 1;28(11):1465-71.

[92] Therapeutic Herbalism p 2-121.

[93] *Reproduced by special permission of the Publisher, Psychological Assessment Resources, Inc., 16204 North Florida Avenue, Lutz, Florida 33549, from the Eating Disorder Inventory-3 by David M. Garner, PhD, Copyright 1984, 1991, 2004, by Psychological Assessment Resources, Inc. (PAR). Further reproduction is prohibited without permission of PAR.*

[94] Nylander I.The feeling of feeling fat and dieting in a school population: An epidemiologic interview investigation. Acta Socio-Medica Scandinavica; 1971; 3:17-26.

[95] Garner, D. M. (2004) Eating Disorder Inventory-3. Professional Manual. Psychological Assessment Resources, Inc.

[96] Crisp, A. H. Sleep, activity, nutrition and mood. British Journal of Psychiatry; 1980;137:1-7.

[97] Linehan MM (1993b) Skills Training Manual for treating borderline personality disorder. New York: Guilford Press.

[98] Safer Dl, Telch CF, AGras WS. Dialectical behavior therapy adapted for bulimia: a case report. Int J Eat Disord. 2001 Jul;30(1):101-6.

[99] Details from this exercise and of case example are composites of many patients and do not apply to any one person.

[100] Kornfield, Jack. The Art of Forgiveness, Lovingkindness, and Peace. 2002. Bantam Books, New York.

[101] Kirsch I, Sapirstein G. Listening to Prozac but hearing placebo: a meta-analysis of antidepressant medication. Prevention & Treatment; epub1998 Jun 28; 1(0002a):1-16.

[102] Walsh BT, Seidman SN, Sysko R, Gould M. Placebo response in studies of major depression: variable, substantial and growing. JAMA, April 10,2002;287(14):1840-7.

[103] Yarnell E, Abascal K. Botanical treatments for depression: Part 1-Herbal correctives for systemic imbalances. Alternative and Complementary Therapies, 2001;7(2):82-87.

[104] Ara DerMarderosian, Lawrence Liberti, John A Beutler, and Constance Grauds, editors. Review of Natural Products. St. John's Wort 11/97. Facts and Comparisons Publishing Group. St. Louis, MO.

[105] Linde K, et al. Br Med J 1996;313(7052):253-8.

[106] www.cochrane.org (Cochrane Library consists of a regularly updated collection of evidence-based medicine databases, including The Cochrane Database of Systematic Reviews).

[107] Harrer G, Hubner WD, Pudzuweit H. Effectiveness and tolerance of the hypericum extract LI 160 compared to maprotiline: a multicenter double-blind study. J Geriatric Psychiatry Neurol 1994;7(suppl 1) S24-8.

[108] Philipp M, Kohnen R, Hiller KO. Hypericum extract versus imipramine or placebo in patients with moderate depression: randomized multicentre study of treatment for eight weeks. BMJ 1999; 319:1534-8.

[109] Wheatley D. LI160, an extract of St. John's wort, versus amitryptyline in mildly to molderately depressed outpatients – a controlled 6-week clinical trial. Pharmacopsychiatry. 1997;30 (suppl 2): 77-80. Medline.

[110] Fava M, Alpert J, Nierenberg AA, et al. A double-blind, randomized trial of St. John's wort, fluoxetine and placebo in major depressive disorder. J. Clin Psychopharmacol. 2005 Oct;25(5):441-7.

[111] Gastpar M, Singer A, Zeller K. Efficacy and tolerability of hyperium extract STW3 in long term treatment with a once-daily dosage in comparison to sertraline. Pharmacopsychiatry, 2005 Mar; 38(2)78-

[112]Linde K, Mulrow CDE, Berner M, Egger M. St John's Wort for depression (Cochrane Review). The Cochrane Library, Issue 2, 2006. Chichester, UK. John Wiley and Sons, Ltd.

[113] Manber R, Allen JJ, Morris MM. Alternative treatments for depression: empirical support and relevance to women. J Clin Psychiatry. 2002 Jul;63(7):628-40.

[114] Szegedi A, Kohnen R, Dienel A, Kieser M. Acute treatment of moderate to severe depression with hypericum extract WS5570 (St. John's wort): randomized controlled double blind non-inferiority trial versus paroxetine. BMJ 2005;330:503 (5 March), doi:10.1136/bmj.38356.655266.82.

[115] Kobak KA, Taylor LV, Warner G, Futterer R. St. John's wort versus placebo in social phobia: results from a placebo-controlled pilot study. J Clin Psychopharmacol. 2005 Feb;25(1):51-8.

[116] Muller T, Mannel M, Murek H, Rahlfs VW. Treatment of somatoform disorders with St. John's wort: a randomized, double-blind and placebo-controlled trial. Evid Based Ment Health. 2005 Feb;8(1):13.

[117] Basch Ethan M, Ulbricht Catherine E (Chief Editors). Natural Standard Herb and Supplement Handbook: The clinical bottom line. 2005. St. Louis, MO. Elsevier Mosby.

[118] Saletu B, Anderer P, DiPadova C, et al. Electrophysiological neuroimaging of the central effects of S-adenosyl-L-Methionine by mapping of electroencephalograms and event-related potentials and low-resolution brain electromagnetic tomography. Am J Clin Nutr 2002 Nov;76(5):1162S-71S.

[119] Bressa GM. S-adenosyl-l-methionine (SAMe) as antidepressant: meta-analysis of clinical studies. Acta Neurol Scand Suppl 1994; 154:7-14.

[120] (www.ahrq.gov)

[121] Alpert JE, Papakostas G, Michoulon D, et al. SAMe as an adjunct for resistant major depressive disorder: an open trial following partial or nonresponse to selective serotonin reuptake inhibitors or venlafaxine. J Clin Psychopharmacol. 2004 Dec; 24(6):661-4.

[122] di Padova C S-adenosylmethionine in the treatment of osteoarthritis. Review of the clinical studies. Am J Med. 1987 Nov 20;83(5A):60-5.

[123] Konig B. A long-term (two years) clinical trial with S-adenosylmethionine for the treatment of osteoarthritis. Am J Med 1987 Nov 20;83(5A):89-94.

[124] Najm WI, Reinsch S, Hoehler F, et al. SAMe versus celecoxib for the treatment of osteoarthritis symptoms:a couble-blind cross-over trial. BMC Musculoskelet Disord. 2004 Feb 26;5:6.

[125] Tavoni A Vitali C, Bombardieri S, Pasero G. Evaluatin of S-adenosylmethionine in primary fibromyalgia. A double-blind crossover study. Am J Med 1987 Nov 20;83(5A):107-10.

102. Jacobsen S, Danneskiold-Samsoe B, Andersen RB. Oral S-adenosylmethionine in primary fibromyalgia. Double-blind clinical evaluation. Scand J Rheumatol. 1991;20(4):294-302.

[126] Chawla RK, Bonkovsky HL, Galambos JT. Biochemistry and pharmacology and SAMe and rationale for its use in liver disease. Drugs 1990;40 Suppl 3:98-110.

[127] Loguercio C, Nardi G, Argenzio F, et al. Effect of SAMe administration on red blood cell cysteine and glutathione levels in alcoholic patients with and without liver disease. Alcohol Alcohol. 1994 Sep;29(5):597-604.

[128] Goren JL, Stoll AL, Damico KE, et al. Bioavailability and lack of toxicity of S-adenosyl-L-methionine (SAMe) in humans. Pharmacotherapy. 2004 Nov; 24(11):1501-7.

[129] Natural Medicine Comprehensive database (see reference above).

[130] Note: there was concern that the use of SAMe might increase levels of homocysteine, which has been implicated in the genesis of heart disease. Recent studies have not shown this to be the case.

[131] http://en.wikipedia.org/wiki/Tryptophan.

[132] U.S. Food and Drug Administration. Center for Food Safety and Applied Nutrition. Feb, 2001. "Information Paper on L-tryptophan and 5-hydroxy-L-tryptophan." www.cfsan.fda.gov/~dms/ds-tryp1.html.

[133] Birdsall TC. 5-Hydroxytryptophan: a clinically effective serotonin precursor. Altern Med Rev. 1998 Aug;3(4):271-80.

[134] Shaw K, Turner, J, Del Mar C. Tryptophan and 5-Hydroxytryptophan for depression. Cochrane Database Syst Rev. 2002;(1):CD003198.

[135] Das YT, Bagchi M, Bagchi D, Preuss HG. Safety of 5-Hydroxy-L-tryptophan. Toxicol Lett. 2004 Apr 15;150(1):111-22.

[136] Kahn RS, Westenberg HG. L-5-hydroxytryptophan in the treatment of anxiety disorders. J Affect Disord. 1985 Mar-Apr;8(2):197-200.

[137] Cangiano C, Ceci F, Cascino A, et al. Eating behavior and adherence to dietary prescriptions in obese adult subjects treated with 5-hydroxytryptophan. Am J Clin Nutr, 1992 Nov; 56(5):863-7.

[138] Cangiano C, Ceci F, Cascino A, et al. Eating behavior and adherence to dietary prescriptions in obese adult subjects treated with 5-hydroxytryptophan. Am J Clin Nutr, 1992 Nov;56(5):863-7.

[139] Cangiano C, Laviano A, Del Ben, M et al. Effects of oral 5-hydroxy-tryptophan on energy intake and macronutrient selection in non-insulin dependent diabetic patients. Int J Obes Relat Metab Disord. 1998 Jul; 22(7):648-54.

[140] Singhal AB, Caviness VS, BEgleiter AF, et al. Cerebral vasoconstriction and stroke after use of serotonergic drugs. Neurology. 2002 Jan 8;58(1):130-3.

[141] Lu K, Gray MA, Oliver C, et al. The acute effects of L-theanine in comparison with alprazolam on anticipatory anxiety in humans. Hum Psychopharmacoll, 2004 Oct; 19(7):457-65.

[142] Kimura K, Ozeki M, Juneja LR, Ohira H. L-Theanine reduces psychological and physiological stress responses. Biol Psychol, 2006 Aug 21; Epub ahead of print.

[143] Blinder BJ, Cumella EJ, Sanathara VA. Psychiatric comorbidities of female inpatients with eating disorders. Psychosom Med 2006 May-Jun;68(3):454-62.

[144] Bulik CM, Klump KL, Thornton L, et al. Alcohol use disorder comorbidity in eating disorders: a multicenter study. J Clin Psychiatry 2004 Jul;65(7):1000-6.

[145] Leonard S, Steiger H, Kao A. Childhood and adulthood abuse in bulimic and nonbulimic women: prevalences and psychological correlates. Int J Eat Disord. 2003 May;33(4):397-405.

[146] Grilo CM, Masheb RM. Childhood psychological, physical, and sexual maltreatment in outpatients with binge eating disorder: frequency and associations with gender, obesity, and eating-related psychopathology. Obes Res. 2001 May;9(5):320-5.

[147] Grilo CM, Masheb RM, Brody M, et al. Childhood maltreatment in extremely obese male and female bariatric surgery candidates. Obes Res. 2005 Jan;13(1):123-30.

[148] Mulvihill D. The health impact of childhood trauma: an interdisciplinary review, 1997-2003. Issues Compr Pediatr Nurs. 2005 Apr-Jun;28(2):115-36.

[149] Gerke CK, Mazzeo SE, Kliewer W. The role of depression and dissociation in the relationship between childhood trauma and bulimic

symptoms among ethnically diverse female undergraduates. Child Abuse Negl. 2006 Oct;30(10):1161-72.

[150] Hoffmann D L. Therapeutic herbalism. A correspondence course in phytotherapy. 1995(4): 2-95.

[151] Levine, Peter. "Waking the Tiger: Healing Trauma." North Atlantic Books, Berkeley, CA. 1997: p. 100

[152] Claes SJ. Corticotropin-releasing hormone in psychiatry: from stress to psychopathology. Trends in Molecular Medicine. Taylor and Francis healthsciences. 2003 ISSN 0785-3890.

[153] Claes SJ. CRH in psychiatry: from stress to psychopathology. Annals of Med 2004. 36(1): 50-61.

[154] Claes SJ. CRH, stress and major depression: a psychobiological interplay Vitam Horm. 2004;69:117-50.

[155] Putignano P, Dubini A, Toja P, et al. Salivary cortisol measurement in normal-weight, obese and anorexic women: comparison with plasma cortisol. Eur J Endocrinol. 2001 Aug; 145(2):165-71.

[156] Martins JM, Trinca A, Afonso A, et al. Psychoneuroendocrine characteristics of common obesity clinical subtypes. Int J Obes Relat Metab Disord. 2001 Jan;25(1):24-32.

[157] Schule C, Sighart C, Hennig J, Laakman G. Mirtazapine in hibits salivary cortisol concentrations in anorexia nervosa. Prog Neuropsychopharmacol Biol Psychiatry. 2006 Aug 30;30(6):1015-9 Epub 2006 Apr.

[158] Zonnevylle-Bender MJ, van Goozen SH, Cohen-Kettenis PT, et al. Adolescent anorexia nervosa patients have a discrepancy between neurophysiological responses and self-reported emotional arousal to psychosocial stress. Psychiatry Res. 2005 May 15;135(1):45-52.

[159] Birketvedt GS, Drivenes E, Agledahl I, et al. Bulimia nervosa – a primary defect in the hypothalamic-pituitary-adrenal axis? Appetite. 2006 Mar;46(2):164-7. Epub 2006 Feb 24.

[160] Krupa D. www.the-aps.org/press/journal/release2-7-02-4.htm.

[161] Troop NA, Holbrey A, Treasure JL. Stress, coping, and crisis support in eating disorders. Int J Eat Disord. 1998 Sep;24(2):157-66.

[162] Soukup VM, Beiler ME, Terrell F. Stress, coping style, and problem solving ability among eating-disordered inpatients. J Clin Psychol. 1990 Sep;46(5):592-9.

[163] Troop NA, Holbrey A, Trowler R, Treasure JL. Ways of coping in women with eating disorders. J Nerv Ment Dis. 1994 Oct;182(10):535-40.

[164] Keel PK, Mitchell JE, Davis TL, Crow SJ. Relationship between depression and body dissatisfaction in women diagnosed with bulimia nervosa. Int J Eat Disord. 2001 Jul;30(1):48-56.

[165] Sinha R, Garcia M, Paliwal P, et al. Stress Induced cocaine craving and HPA axis responses predict cocaine relapse outcomes. Arch of Gen Psych (in press).

[166] Al' Absi M, Hatsukami D, Davis GL. Attenuated adrenocorticotrophic responses to psychological stress are associated with early smoking relapse. Psychopharmacology. Springer-Verlag 2005. 10.1007/s00213-005-2225-3.

[167] Claes SJ. CRH in psychiatry: from stress to psychopathology. Annals of Med 2004. 36(1): 50-61.

[168] Brady KT, Sinha R. Co-occurring mental and substance use disorders: the neurobiological effects of chronic stress. Am J Psychiatry 2005;162:1483-93.

[169] Norman Pecoraro, Faith Reyes, Francisca Gomez, Aditi Bhargava and Mary F. Dallman. Chronic Stress Promotes Palatable Feeding, which Reduces Signs of Stress: Feedforward and Feedback Effects of Chronic Stress Endocrinology Vol. 145, No. 8 3754-3762.

[170] Dallman MF, Pecoraro N, Akana SF, et al. Chronic stress and obesity: a new view of "comfort food." PNAS 100:11696-11701, 2003.

[171] Yeomans MR,Gray RW. Opioid peptides and the control of human ingestive behaviour Neurosci Biobehav Rev. 2002 Oct;26(6):713-28.

[172] Gluck ME, Geliebter A, Lorence M. Cortisol stress response is positively correlated with central obesity in obese women with binge eating disorder (BED) before and after cognitive-behavioral treatment. Ann N Y Acad Sci. 2004 Dec; 1032:202-7.

[173] Natural Standard Herb and Supplement Handbook. Editors: Basch EM, Ulbricht CE. Elsevier Mosby pp335-47. St. Louis MO. 2005.

[174] http://en.wiktionary.org/wiki/neurasthenia.

[175] Unless otherwise cited, information about R. rosea was obtained from the excellent review article: Brown RP, Gerbarg PL, Ramazanov Z. Rhodiola rosea: a Phytomedicinal Overview. Herbalgram. 2002;56:40-52.

[176] Natural Standard Herb and Supplement Handbook. Editors: Basch EM, Ulbricht CE. Elsevier Mosby St. Louis MO: pp 35-45.

[177] Reprinted from *Plum Village Chanting and Recitation Book* (2000) by Thich Nhat Hahn with permission of Parallax Press, Berkeley, California, www.parallax.org

[178] Pop-Jordanova N. Psychological characteristics and biofeedback mitigation in preadolescents with eating disorders. Pediatr Int. 2000 Feb;42(1):76-81.

[179] Esplen MJ, Garfinkel PE, Olmsted M, et al. A randomized controlled trial of guided imagery in bulimia nervosa. Psychol Med. 1998 Nov;28(6):1347-57.

[180] Laessle RG, Beaumont PJ, Butow P, et al. A comparison of nutritional management with stress management in the treatment of bulimia nervosa. Br J Psychiatry. 1991 Aug; 159:250-61.

[181] Kirsch I, Montgomery G, Sapirstein G. Hypnosis as an adjunct to cognitive-behavioral psychotherapy: a meta-analysis. J Consult Clin Psychol 1995;63:214-20.

[182] Stanton HE, Hypnotic relaxation and the reduction of sleep onset insomnia. Int J Psychosom. 1989;36(1-4):64-8.

[183] Benson H, Beary JF, Carol MP: The relaxation response. Psychiatry 37:37-46, 1974.

[184] Ernst E, Rand JL, Stevinson C. Complementary therapies for depression. Arch Gen Psychiatry. 1998;55:1026-32.

[185] Authors not listed. Integration of behavioral and relaxation approaches into the treatment of chronic pain and insomnia. NIH Technology Assessment Panel on Integration of Behavioral and Relaxation Approaches into the treatment of chronic pain and insomnia. 1994 Jul24;JAMA 276(4):313.

[186] Kirsch I, Montgomery, Sapirstein G. Hypnosis as an adjunct to cognitive-behavioral psychotherapy: a meta-analysis. J of Consulting and clinical psych. 1995: 63(2):214-20.

[187] Jorm AF, Christensen, Griffiths KM, Rodgers B. Depression and the community. Effectiveness of complementary and self-help treatments for depression. The Med J of Australia. 20 May 2002:176(10 Suppl): S84-95.

[188] Kabat-Zinn J, Massion AO, Kristeller J, et al. Effectiveness of a meditation-based stress reduction program in the treatment of anxiety disorders. Am J Psychiatry. 1992 Jul; 149(7):936-43.

[189] Miller JJ, Fletcher K, Kabat-Zinn J. Three-year follow-up and clinical implications of a mindfulness meditation-based stress reduction intervention in the treatment of anxiety disorders. Gen Hosp Psychiatry 1995; 17, 192-200.

[190] Teasdale JD, Moore RG, Hayhurst H, et al. Metacognitive awareness and prevention of relapse in depression: empirical evidence. J Consult Clin Psychol. 2002 Apr; 70(2):275-87.

[191] Woolery A, Myers H, Sternlieb B, et al. A yoga intervention for young adults with elevated symptoms of depression. Altern Ther. Mar/Apr 2004; 10(4):60-2.

[192] Janakiramaiah N, Gangadhar BN, Naga Venkatesha Murthy PJ, et al. Antidepressant efficacy of Sudarshan Kriya Yoga in melancholia: a randomized comparison with electroconvulsive therapy and imipramine. J Affect Disord 2000; 57:255-57.

[193] Shannahoff-Khalsa DS. Clinical case report: efficacyof yogic techniques in the treatment of obsessive compulsive disorders. Intern J Neuroscience, 1996, Vol 85:1-17.

[194] Shaffer HJ, LaSalvia TA, Stein JP. Original research: comparing hatha yoga with dynamic group psychotherapy for enhancing methadone maintenance treatment; a randomized clinical trial. Altern Ther in Health and Medicine Jul 97;3(4).

[195] Sharma K, Shuka V. Rehabilitation of drug-addicted persons: the experience of the Nav Chetna Center in India. Bull Narc. 1988;15:43-9.

[196] Netz Y, Lidor R. Mood alterations in mindful versus aerobic exercise modes. J Psychol. 2003 Sep;137(5):405-19.

[197] www.qigonginstitute.org.

[198] www.zerobalancing.com.

[199] Wardell DW, Engebretson J. Biological correlates of Reiki Touch(sm) Healing. J Adv Nurs. 2001 Feb;33(4):439-45.

[200] Olson K, Hanson J, Michaud M. A phase II trial of Reiki for the management of pain in advanced cancer patients. J Pain Symptom Manage, 2003 Nov;26(5):990-7.

[201] Shore AG. Long-term effects of energetic healing on symptoms of psychological depression and self-perceived stress. Altern Ther Health Med. 2004 May-Jun;10(3):42-8.

[202] Hagemaster J. Use of therapeutic touch in treatment of drug addictions. Holist Nurs Pract. 2000 Apr;14(3):14-20.

[203] Laidlaw TM, Naito A, Dwivedi P, et al. The influence of 10 min of the JOhrei healing method on laboratory stress. Complement Ther Med 2006 Jun;14(2):127-32.

[204] Elkins G, Fajab MH, Marcus J. Complementary and alternative medicine use by psychiatric inpatients. Psychol Rep, 2005 Feb;96(1):163-6.

[205] Field T, Hernandez-Reif M, Diego M, et al. Cortisol decreases and serotonin and dopamine increase following massage therapy. Int J Neurosci. 2005 Oct;115(10):1397-413.

[206] (no authors listed) Anorexia Nervosa Symptoms are Reduced by Massage therapy. Eat. Disor. 2001 Winter;9(4):289-99.

[207] Field T, Schanberg S, Kuhn C., et al. Bulimic adolescents benefit from massage thera py. Adolescence 1998 Fall; 33(131):555-63.

[208] Field T, Hernandez-REif M, Diego M, et al. Cortisol decreases and serotonin and dopamine increase following massage therapy. Int J Neurosci, 2005 Oct; 115(10):1397-1413.

[209] Field T, Grizzle N, Scafidi F, Schanberg S. Massage and relaxation therapies' effects on depressed adolescent mothers. Adolescence. 1996 Winter; 31(124): 903-11.

[210] Collinge W. Ther Amreican Holistic Health Association Complete Guide to Alternative Medicine. Warner Books, New York. 1996.

[211] WHO. Constitution of the World Health Organziation, Geneva, 1946. Accessed October 30, 2006. www.wikipedia.com.

[212] Flexner A. Medical Education in the United States and Canada. 1910; (http://www.carnegiefoundation.org/elibrary/docs/flexner_report.pdf).

[213] Beinfield H, Korngold, E. Between Heaven and Earth: A guide to Chinese medicine. 1991. New York, New York. Ballantine Books, The Random House Publishing Group.

[214] This terminology was taught to author through a personal communication by Stephen Gurgevich, PhD. www.tranceformation.com.

[215] Robinson TN, Chang JY, Haydel KF, Killen JD. Overweight concerns and body dissatisfaction among third-grade children: the impacts of ethnicity and socioeconomic status. J Pediatr. 2001 Feb;138(2):181-7.

[216] Lad, V. 1998. The Complete Book of Ayurvedic Home Remedies. New York, Three Rivers Press: 15-29.

[217] Lad, V. 1998. The Complete Book of Ayurvedic Home Remedies. New York, Three Rivers Press: 28.

[218] www.wikipedia.com.

[219] Chakra information obtained in a personal communication with Rosalyn Bruyere, well known energy healer, teacher and author. See www.rosalynbruyere.org.

[220] Collinge W. AHHA Guide to Alternative Medicine, 1996. p. 13-43 Chapter 2. New York, NY. Warner Books.

[221] Smith Ca, Hay PP. Acupuncture for depression. Cochrane Database Syst Rev. 2005 Apr 18;(2):CD4046.

[222] Mukaino Y, Park J, White A, Ernst E. The effectiveness of acupuncture for depression – a systematic review of randomized controlled trials. Acupunct Med. 2005 Jun;23(2):70-6.

[223] Gallagher SM, Allen JJ, Hitt SK, et al. Six-month depression relapse rates among women treated with acupuncture. Complement Ther Med. 2001 Dec;9(4):216-8.

[224] Lipton DS, Brewington V, Smith M. Acupuncture for crack-cocaine detoxification: experimental evaluation of efficacy. J Subst Abuse Treat. 1994 May-Jun;11(3):205-15.

[225] Bullock ML, Kiresuk TJ, Pheley AM, et al. Auricular acupuncture in the treatment of cocaine abuse. A study of efficacy and dosing. J Subst Abuse Treat. 1999 Jan;16(1):31-8.

[226] Personal communication: Paige Peters, L.Ac. Sierra Tucson, 2005.

[227] For more in depth information about the five elements in TCM, please see: Beinfield H, Korngold, E. Between Heaven and Earth: A guide to

Chinese medicine. 1991. New York, New York. Ballantine Books, The Random House Publishing Group.

Printed in the United States
101438LV00001B/241-333/A

9 781432 701918